What others are saying about this book...

"Judy has shown that an ordinary person can discover how to be a survivor. In *Healthy Mind·Healthy Body* she shows how survival comes from a spirit of independence, outward searching, inner self-examination, a willingness to learn and change, playfulness, and creating your own self-healing plan."

Al Siebert, Ph.D.
Author of *The Survivor Personality*

"Subtle but powerful. Read these words and meditate on them."

Freida Grell, M.D.

"Enlightening, captivating, enjoyable sense of openness. Thinking rarely shared."

Agnes Abel, M.A.
Family Counselor

Healthy Mind · Healthy Body

Using Your Mind Power to Stay Healthy and Overcome Illness

by
Judy Pearson
Edited by Jean Celia

Awe Books Publishing

Hillsboro, Oregon

Cover design: Tim Oakley Studios
Editor: Jean Celia
Typesetting: Terri Walker
Photos in book: Starlight Photography - Tammi Clark
Photo on back cover: Pumpkin Ridge Photography

Printed in the United States of America

Publisher's Cataloging-in-Publication Data

Pearson, Judith A.
   Healthy Mind·Healthy Body: using your mind power to stay healthy and overcome illness / Judith A. Pearson.-1st ed.
      p. cm.
   Includes: Index; bibliography; illustrations.
   Preassigned LCCN: 94-071480
   ISBN 0-9635179-0-2
   1. Mind and body. 2. Mental healing. 3. Meditation.
   4. Affirmations. 5. Stress.(psychology). 6. Cancer-Patients-United States- Biography. I. Title.
RZ401.P42 1994
615.8'51-dc20   [BCS0016]

Published by:
Awe Books Publishing
2459 SE Tualatin Valley Hwy., #108
Hillsboro, Oregon 97123-7919
(503) 640-3208

Acknowledgments

This has been a pleasure to write, thanks to the help of family, friends, advisors and associates, among them: Ed, Susan, Ron, Carrie, Wensdai, and Naomi Pearson; Heather Kibbey; Jean Celia; Mary Midkiff; Don Wright; Rev. Jody Stevenson; Dottie Walters; and Colleen Watkins.

And to the talented cover designer and illustrator Tim Oakley, thanks for a job well done.

Table of Contents

Part I 11
Introduction 12
Sitting On A Tack: My Wake-Up Call 13

Part II 32
The Seven Character Roles We Play in Life's Theater 33
Gracie Gossip 35
Ulla Dunnit 39
Waukeen Wounded 43
Super Stella 47
Freda Fine 51
Nanna Yabut 54
Nurse Cratchit 57

Part III 61
The 3 A's of Healthy, Happy Living 63
The 3 A's for Gracie Gossip 70
The 3 A's for Ulla Dunnit 72
The 3 A's for WaukeenWounded 74
The 3 A's for Nurse Cratchit 77
The 3 A's for Super Stella 78
The 3 A's for Freda Fine 80
The 3 A's for Nanna Yabut 81

Part IV 83
Mini-bite Insights to a Healthier You 84
Resolutions 85
Cleaning the Closet 86
Ledge Living 89
Trying on Many Coats 91

No Pain, No Gain! Push it! Push it! 94
10 Amusing Excuses for Not Exercising 97
High Hopes 98
Laugh At Yourself 102
Devoted Eating 105
Devoted Eating Meditation 106
The Wizardry of Awe Counting 108
Five Steps to Awesomeness: 111
Leaning Out 112
Pricing Success...116
Go With The Flow 118

Part V 120
Meditations for the Stressful Times 121
Meditation for the Stressful Times of Employment.......130
A Meditation for the Stressful Times of Divorce............132
A Meditation for the Stressful Times at the Holidays ...134
A Meditation for the Stressful Times of
    Personal Illness or Injury...135
Meditation for the Stressful Times of Forgiveness.........137
Decide to Forgive 139
Meditation for the Stressful Times of Change
    in the Family 140
Meditation for the Stressful Times of Transition
    of a Loved One..142
Meditation for the Stressful Times with Finances 144
Meditation for the Stressful Time of Vacations 146
Meditation for the Stressful Times of
    Health Challenges of a Family Member 148
Meditation for the Stressful Times of Success................150

Resources and Bibliography 158

*This book is dedicated to Ian Alexander Pearson,
George and Anna White, Monty White, and
John Thomas White, who taught me valuable lessons
about how to truly live life by following my bliss.*

About the Author

Judy Pearson is a professional speaker, seminar leader, and consultant. She presents empowering keynote talks and workshops to assist people in accessing their own body intelligence to stay well and live happier and healthier lives. Judy shares the experience of overcoming cancer twice using the power of the mind-body-spirit. Combining humor, true stories and useful take-home information, she inspires the audience to take charge of their well being.

Judy's early years were spent in Red Bluff, California. She is a Shasta College graduate, studied philosophy and the human mind. Her careers have included usher, retail clerk, teacher's aide, teacher of drawing and painting, business owner, spiritual consultant, artist, school photographer, professional writer, wife and mother.

Foreword

There is no doubt that the body and the mind are connected. When the body gets sick the mind has to do something about it. The mind is supposed to get the message and take action by changing negative attitudes into positive ones. We simply have to stop blaming ourselves or our parents for the way we turned out. Every one of us can make mental changes that affect the body. Obviously we all must eat better, avoid toxins and drugs, and exercise a little but we have all the evidence we need that the mind can rid the body of diseases.

Judy Pearson shows us how in this easy to read and understandable book. She takes us by the hand and gives us the tools to change our attitudes, and then, voila, behavior changes. I like the idea that she is promoting: "I am my best friend. I must be nice to myself." Some of her ideas are simplistic and even a little corny, but when one is dealing with a potentially fatal disease like cancer, whatever works. Ten years ago a book like this would have been laughed off the shelves. Her quotes are appropriate and thought provoking. Examples and humor abound.

You don't have to be slapped with a nasty diagnosis to start to change your distorted perceptions of yourself and your world. Read this book, follow her suggestions, and report back when you are ninety years old that you have had a good life.

Lendon Smith, M.D.

Part I

Introduction

It may be an accident, divorce, or the death of a loved one. Or it could be that special moment you experience extraordinary music for the first time, or astounding insight from a great book, or a million other ways that sets you on a new path to wanting a greater experience of life.

One minute we believe life is a struggle, we are all victims, and that spirit is out there somewhere, left for the spiritual folks. We think that life is just a place to survive for a while, a place to wait for your space in heaven.

Then one day life becomes painfully uncomfortable. You have a choice to stay in the pain or do something about it. You discover that life is in the here and now, that this is the moment to enjoy, and tomorrow is a bonus, that laughing is the best thing people can do for themselves and everyone around them. Old ways of doing things seem obsolete, old friends are seen in a different light, and life just becomes lighter and easier.

In the following chapter "Sitting On A Tack," I share my story of recovery in the hope of giving you more confidence, courage, and the advantage of knowing you are not alone in the process of life. You too can learn to use your mind-body and spirit to stay well and/or overcome any illness or other challenge.

Sitting On A Tack:
My Wake-Up Call

"The only known cure for fear is faith."

Lena Kellogg Sadler

I stared in silent horror, freezing, as the words "tumor the size of a grapefruit," "cancer in the third degree," "chemotherapy," rolled across my doctor's desk at my post-hysterectomy consultation. I hadn't been sick, no colds, hardly ever got the flu. Life was filled with the usual ups and downs, but...cancer?

Timidly I asked, "Are there alternatives to chemotherapy?" His sunken reply: "No. The hysterectomy didn't take care of everything. We could still lose you." Through a stir of mixed feelings—everything from "What makes me think little ol' me knows anything?" to "Doctors know everything"—one thought pushed its way out, as I said, "My mind doesn't think chemotherapy is good for me." With the assurance of the medical profession behind him, the doctor's words cut like a knife. "Your mind has nothing to do with it. Your first scheduled chemotherapy session is two weeks from today."

Maybe the doctor was right. What made me think I knew anything about getting over cancer? I'd never heard anyone say they had been cured of cancer. But I was fighting mad. "Your mind has nothing to do with it." How dare he say such a thing?

Little did I know this was exactly what I needed to hear.

Driving home, I made up my mind. I didn't know what I was going to do, but it wasn't going to be the chemical "quick cure."

Did you ever notice how some people often turn into ostriches in the wake of a crisis? My husband Ed had had his head under the hood of a car at every turning point during the nineteen years of our marriage, and this was no exception. "Chemotherapy starts in two weeks. I've decided not to go," I announced. He drew his head of thick gray hair up from the motor and our eyes met. With a plea in his voice, he said, "So what are you going to do—die?" At that moment I realized my fear and depression were having an impact, not only on me but on the people I loved.

A picture flashed through my mind of the smell of the hospital, and sick people with dark circles under their eyes lining the hall of the chemotherapy clinic. My choice was reconfirmed. No chemical quick fix for me. I knew that if I continued down the path my life had taken, the doctors would just continue to remove pieces of Judy until there weren't any more pieces to remove.

Panic pushed me. I felt tired, depressed, and aching from the hysterectomy. Ed chauffeured me from one "professional" to another. They suggested vitamins, coffee enemas, trips to Mexico, diets, adjustments, and massages. One even suggested I try Indian sweats. Others suggested I investigate the spiritual side of things. There seemed to be some validity in each of these options, but nothing caught my attention and felt right. I wanted the answer right now, yet I was running away from the available answer of chemotherapy. It was like trying to catch a fly in a whirlwind. Every method of healing I explored kept pointing to one factor: if I didn't *believe* in the process, it probably wasn't going to work. Clenching fear so tightly kept me from accepting anything but my fear.

When I called the American Cancer Society (ten years ago), they said they didn't believe that diet had any role to play in getting well and staying well. Their only suggestion? "Chemotherapy." We have come a long way in the last ten years. The American Cancer Society now endorses a low-fat, high-fiber diet as a prevention practice.

What drove me to find an alternative healing was a combination of circumstances. I had read and re-read enough to be dangerous. Self-help books, healthy diet, and positive-mind articles lined my shelves. I read but did nothing. Most importantly, subconsciously I had decided that enough was enough.

When I was nineteen I had had a cancerous tumor removed from a saliva gland. At nineteen I had everything going for me. After graduating from high school, I was in my first year of cosmetology. (Everyone went to beauty school that year.) During the summer break I complained of an earache. My mom arranged for a doctor's appointment for me, and wham-bam the next day I was in the hospital for major surgery. The following day, my head was swollen from my ear to my shoulder and I had no neck. My face was deformed, all my facial muscles on one side didn't work, my eye didn't close, my mouth, eyebrow and nose had moved over to my good side. My first look in the mirror was a traumatic, horrifying event. Mom could never hide her feelings very well. Her red, wet eyes were a give-away to the fact that I had cancer. The doctors said "that there was no proven treatment for this type of cancer." The advice was to leave it alone.

I came home in bandages. I was afraid, I knew cancer meant death. I made out a hand-written will, designating who would get my pleated skirts, Elvis record, watch, and a statue of Mary that I sometimes prayed to — in other words, my valuables.

In a month the swelling went down, and a friend took me out to see a movie. An old boyfriend, startled by my appearance, blurted out, "You look like Frankenstein." He called the next day to apologize but I knew what I looked like. Not wanting to upset my family, I spent months in the back of the living room exercising my face while everyone watched television.

I soon learned who my friends were. People for various reasons, mostly fear, never came to see me again. One friend, Ed, who later became my life-long friend and husband, visited me often enough for me to think things were going to be all right. I was determined to live life differently.

I wish I could say my childhood home and family was filled with love every minute. It wasn't. My mother dominated our lives. She loved to control and controlled to love. I recall life went pretty well until I reached puberty. Then all hell broke loose. As I look back, I realize the forbidden box in the bottom dresser drawer that held the newspaper clipping about a little two year old who had been molested (I found out later that was me) added to her guilt and influenced her judgment in child rearing. Her insecurities and low self-esteem came crashing down around my ears as I developed into a woman. I felt trapped, with little say in what I wanted to do. I never knew when I came home from school what her mood would be. Although she was never diagnosed, she showed signs of manic-depressive behavior. My father left all the child rearing to his wife. I learned to survive amidst verbal and physical abuse. I was sure the abuse was my fault until I read John Bradshaw's book *Home Coming* where he talks about alcohol, sexual, verbal, and physical abuse in dysfunctional families.

Six years went flying by. After the operation, my face healed. I married my boyfriend Ed and life was filled with two small babies. I was busy enjoying life. In a small town where everyone knows everyone's business, the doctor's receptionist was a family friend. She said, "You are doing remarkably well." I said, "Yes?" "Don't tell anyone, but when you got the `Big C' the doctors only gave you two years." I was astonished. Yet I was healthy and happy and life goes on, so I buried those thoughts of fear and went on living.

Now I am forty and life is starting to get rolling again. We had just sold a dump truck that kept Ed busy 15 hours a day on his days off...when he wasn't on duty 24 hours as a firefighter. I was trying to be super mom, filling in for the time that Ed wasn't taking with our two teenagers in basketball, soccer, dance, baseball, and all those other things. (Well, all I really had to say was 'teenagers,' right?) I know now that I was again feeling trapped and wasn't making any time for me to be alone or get to know myself.

Despite my doubt that God even existed, I was being guided. Seven years earlier my aunt Daisy handed me several *Science of Mind* magazines about positive thinking and the spiritual power of the mind. Occasionally I would thumb through them and find some element of truth — a spiritual message that I didn't fully understand but was somehow comforting. I found myself responding with, "Uh huh, that's right, that's nice."

Six months prior to this crisis, Ed and I were watching an evening television informational show featuring the book *Recalled By Life*, introducing a mysterious diet called macrobiotics, developed in the U.S. by Micho Kishi. Ed is not one to send for anything, nor was he at all interested in changing his diet. But he suggested I might be interested in this program, so I took his advice and sent for the information.

It was the story of Dr. Anthony Satillaro, who had cured himself of cancer through diet and lifestyle changes. Dr. Satillaro was diagnosed with cancerous tumors throughout his body. Traditional medicine had given up. He had surgeries and therapy, yet his doctors had given him only a few months to live. Dr. Satillaro is the President of Methodist Hospital in Philadelphia and steeped in the ways of western medicine. Diagnosed with cancerous tumors throughout his body, his testicles removed, his father dying of cancer a month prior, Dr. Satillaro's story unfolded. I read the remarkable story of his picking up two hitchhikers who introduced him to the macrobiotic diet and lifestyle change that within a year gave him more energy, his body free from all the cancerous tumors. His health and energy were restored to a degree higher than he had ever experienced before.

An envelope with the information arrived in my mail, I glanced at it, then I tucked it into that overflowing bookcase, burdened with all my other good intentions.

Ed asked if the information from that television show had ever arrived. I found the envelope and made a call. On the other end of the phone line, the receptionist at the macrobiotic center invited us for dinner so we might taste the food and meet people who were eating this (very peculiar) way and living healthy lives.

When we arrived at the dinner we were greeted by our host in a modest home and led toward the aroma of a wonderful barbecue in the back yard. Ed and I had just stepped into the twilight zone of the 1960's. Everyone there was 20 years younger, dressed in Birkenstocks, cotton T-shirts, wrinkled clothing, and feasting on something foreign to our lifestyle, called vegetables. Mark, a young Dutchman, and Anna, an unusually quiet Italian, were college students who had studied the macrobiotic philosophy and diet with Micho Kishi.

We saw corn on the cob, carrots with burdock (a root that looks like tree bark) and strange sea vegetables (Kombu dishes), delicious beans and brownies for dessert. Ed and I exchanged glances, shrugged and dug in. We had both been brought up on the American diet of meat and potatoes. Vegetables came from a can and hit the plate in half cup portions. This food was fresh, alive, and tasted wonderful. Could it be that fresh, alive food would make the body fresh and alive? Before we left that evening we set a time to consult with them on this change in lifestyle that we planned to undertake and explore.

I knew the mind and the body had a connection to being healthy. Logically I knew it. Knowing it in your head is one thing and putting it to practical use in your life is entirely another. I asked myself, "How do I include this in real life?"

Mark and Anna shared the philosophy and practice of macrobiotics. The idea that eating is a spiritual experience of thanks and awe at the wonder of nature's process of growth and supply gave me pause. The value of clean, fresh, organic foods, whole grains, and fish and chicken without chemicals started to make sense. The saying "What we put into life is what we get out," had new meaning: "What you put in your body affects the mind and body...so what you put in your mouth is what you get out of life."

I took a few lessons in the art of macrobiotic cooking and visited the group for a few more dinners to get the hang of it. What would I do with a family who ate only red meat, turned their noses up at fish...thought pasta was life and scoffed at rice and beans?

My family had good reason to be concerned. After all, my reputation as a cook preceded me. There was the time the oven broiler caught fire and filled our tiny apartment with smoke as I attempted the difficult, challenging task (well, for me it was) of baking refrigerator biscuits. Then there was "clippie spinach." Clippies are little clips used to pin hair in place when you part and section it off for cutting or curling. I had just given myself a permanent wave and taken the rods and clippies out. Gathering spinach from our garden, I brought it in to wash and laid it down near the sink over some hair clippies. Everyone laughed when my brother was heard to say, "What's this?" as he held his fork high. Someone told me that you could take the gas out of beans by adding baking soda. I failed to hear the part about rinsing them off before you cook them! No one was brave enough to try the beans. So we ordered in fried chicken. When I started this new cooking quest, my teenagers, Susan and Ron, would peek into the kitchen and make a decision. "Dad's cooking? All right!" or "Mom's cooking? Oh my God! No...no...no thanks. I'll catch a hamburger on the way to the game tonight." That left dear, sweet Ed to experiment on.

"Learn to get in touch with silence within yourself and know that everything in this life has a purpose. There are no mistakes, coincidences; all events are blessings given to us to learn from."

Elizabeth Kubler-Ross

When my crisis hit, I felt an urge to get in touch with the spiritual side of life. As one of my clients recently said, "I've made an appointment with the pastor--but they don't know anything about healing, they just give it good lip service." The idea that the church I had known actually held any answers seemed far-fetched. Why not try something different? I remembered Aunt Daisy's *Science of Mind Magazines*, and somehow my typical excuse ("I don't like to get up on

Sunday morning") evaporated as my car approached Portland, Oregon's Church of Religious Science.

"Sitting on a Tack" was Rev. Lynne Lowe's talk title that fateful Sunday morning. Every cancer patient's question, "Why me?" was answered as I listened. Life's experiences are always teaching us, and sometimes getting our attention is painful. This philosophy of taking responsibility for my life, co-creating life with Spirit, rang true for me. I was receiving a wake-up call. Hello. Hello.

I had stepped onto the path of a journey that changed my life forever. I took cooking classes, seminars, workshops, and read books on health, nutrition, spiritual awareness, philosophy, and psychology. I kept coming back to an underlying theme: Our minds are creative, and as we think, so we create. Philosopher Ernest Holmes said, "The activity of our mind is thought. We are always acting because we are always thinking." Did I create my cancerous state?

I started noticing how I had turned life-enhancing decisions over to others, and how self-doubt kept me down. Negative thoughts had been killing me, literally, from the inside out. I had been Super-Mom, mind-reader, chauffeur, and chief bottle washer, always leaving myself for last, but still the feelings of resentment, anger, fear and guilt cropped up whenever I helped others at the expense of my own self, at the expense of acknowledging my needs. Day by day, I had to choose to deserve good things in my life. I had to rebuild Judy with a new foundation of trust and honesty if I was ever to find a doctor or any other practitioner I could trust.

Even as I rebuilt myself, the dark side of my thoughts operated on fear. What if this philosophy of mind-body connection and the idea of making yourself well by changing diet and lifestyle habits with your mind is full of beans? What if my surgeon is right and chemotherapy is the only answer? What if...What if... Stubborn and scared, I had given up on doctors. It had been months since I consulted with Mark and Anna. As I followed the diet, I kept thinking, "I can do this by myself." I was telling myself, Mark, and every-one else, for a year now, "I'm fine." I was denying what was happening to my body. "I'm fine" was my defensive tactic to keep from moving forward with any kind of treatment. Never mind the piercing pain in my side, or that I was feeling tired all the time. I stopped looking for medical help. The yellow pages were worn out trying to find the right practitioner. Numbers of doctors, chiropractors, naturopathic doctors, and counselors, to avoid law suits, had a standard answer I was afraid I would hear again, the dreaded word "chemotherapy."

But the shower drain with its harvest of hair and the body looking back in the mirror revealed what my friends had tried to tell me and I had denied for a solid year. I had lost fifty pounds, my 5 feet 9 inches frame weighed a hundred and twenty pounds. My eyes were sunken, my skin was gray. I looked like a starving refugee, and my flesh hung on my bones. Looking at the hair I held between my fingers, a cold, hard feeling in my stomach, I had to face facts: I needed help.

Crying, I fell to my knees. "I give up, God. I give it up to you, God; please help me," and I heard, "Right where the pain seems to operate, the presence of God is." Pain and fear create the turning point that makes us move. I resolved to find a doctor, trusting that no matter what it looked like, God was in charge, directing and guiding, and not even doctors were immune to this guidance. Manifestation takes place when we let go and release fear. That evening I had a call from Mark, recommending a naturopathic physician, Dr. René Espy. "She's a woman!" I thought. "This is good; she'll be gentle and thoughtful, letting me have a say in my healing. This is perfect. Thank you, God." Dr. René, however, had the same answer: "Chemotherapy must be recommended, and I think we can work at building up your body and rejuvenating your liver." (This was apparently the cause of the sideache.)

Once a week I went to her for a combination of kinesiology treatments, chiropractic adjustments and supplements. Kinesiology was the weirdest. Dr. René had me hold my arm straight out and resist a downward movement of slight pressure to determine the weaker points in the body and decide what supplements and or adjustments would assist the body in getting well. It looked pretty hocus-pocus to me. Yet it did begin to make sense that she was treating the whole body, not one symptom. My severely damaged liver responded slowly. The dent in my checkbook was getting larger, while I wasn't feeling much better. Weeks, months went by. The gentle, thoughtful manner of Dr. René stopped abruptly.

"You are not responding to these treatments," she said. "You have cancer in your liver; you have been maintaining a survival mode. You cannot afford to go on like this." My heart sank with her words, "I don't know what to do for you." With her pen poised on her prescription pad, she said, "I want you to go get this book and tape, *You Can Heal Your Life*, by Louise Hay. You probably won't do this; you will probably quit after a day or two. But I want you to listen to this tape twice every day for a month and read the book." But I would prove her wrong. Her phrase "you probably won't do this" triggered the fight in me again.

"Forgiveness is the key to action and freedom."

Hannah Arendt

Louise Hay's soft, powerful words played in my head, "Your beliefs and thoughts create disease; new thoughts can change the condition. It's only a thought you need to change. Learn to love yourself unconditionally, forgive, let go of fear, guilt and worry."

I practiced forgiving my parents, and even forgiving the people I had never met who had affected my life. My doubts and I were becoming friends, or at least getting used to each other. Could this cassette tape make any difference? I was willing to try anything. Fear dissolved when I acknowledged my beliefs as thoughts that I can change. This felt manageable, not so overwhelming. Change a thought — instead of trying to take on the cancer.

I couldn't change the past, I may not be able to change the future and be cancer free, but forgiving each moment brought me peace of mind. The confusing messages I received as a child — "What makes you think you can control anything?" "Oh, what's the use?" "Life isn't worth the struggle," "Just getting by in life is a struggle," "You can't change anything so don't even try" — no longer served me. I let them go. Deliberately. Consciously. In order to live, happy and healthy.

Weeks passed. My body improved as my spirit improved. Digesting food, thinking clearly, having more energy, and best of all, brushing my hair and having a clean brush, were rewards of my efforts to heal my body and mind from the inside out.

"Attitude is Environment"

Anonymous

As I was doing all this stuff to get healthier, I kept noticing my attitude...I discovered all kinds of characters or roles I was playing that kept me from getting well. At first I ignored them; after all, we don't want negatives in our lives. We must focus on the positive. And yet, there are lessons to be learned...not through fear and denial but by acceptance and love. Denial is not only a river in Egypt, it is alive and operating in our lives.

I began to pay attention to how these characters, or roles that I played, ran my life. When I tried to ignore them, they seemed to act like a banished kid: the more he or she is ignored, the bigger the ruckus. When I acknowledged and accepted the characters that were running my life I began to love them and understand how they helped me and hindered me. I identified them and gave them names, as you will see in Part 3.

While it may seem my transformation was a long process with many starts and dead ends, in truth it wasn't. A year after going to Dr. Rene I began to realize I had recovered my health. Now, more than ten years later, I enjoy a healthy, happy, vibrant life. My transformation was perfect for me, with just the right amount of time, people and situations involved. The time it took and every step along the way was necessary for me to reveal the truth of who I am, a Spirit, here on earth to share my Spirit with everyone else's Spirit. The moment I changed my thinking, and I dared to affirm "Chemotherapy isn't necessarily the answer for me!" my mind-body-spirit began to work in harmony, guiding me to the perfect answer.

I was back three years later to visit the physician who initially recommended chemotherapy. Tests showed no signs of cancer. He commented on how healthy I looked, "You look great," he said. "Why haven't you been in sooner?" I explained my new diet and change in lifestyle, and especially how *diet, exercise, meditation,* and *spiritual awareness* had become a part of my everyday life. He listened patiently, but when I finished, he said, "That's all well and good, but I don't believe you can get well that way." His prescription was still chemotherapy. Even with the proof sitting in front of him!

For just a moment, the old questions and feelings of confusion welled up. But I remembered a meditation I had experienced recently. In it, I *visualized* a healthy body. I was relaxing, letting go. Slowly a seagull circled into the picture. When it landed, I read the sign it carried in its beak: "You are healed." This time I had no more questions. My mind, body and soul knew the truth.

Sitting on a tack called cancer was the best thing that ever happened to me. Uphill challenges brought lifestyle changes. Lifestyle changes helped me to accomplish what I didn't dare dream of only a few short years before.

In a nutshell, this was my new plan for a new Judy. Take what you need, change what you want to change, and listen to your inner guidance. Here are some suggestions I have found helpful:

1. **Diet:** A Macrobiotic Diet in modification and/or the American Cancer Society's Cancer Prevention Diet. Find your style and make gradual change. Eat plenty of low fat-high fiber, carbohydrates, fresh vegetables and fruit. Get your food directly from the earth. Dr. Lendon Smith who wrote *Feed Yourself Right* says, "Eat foods that rot...and eat them before they do."

2. **Exercise:** I still don't like to "exercise" but I love to walk. My goal is to walk 4 miles a day. I can tell myself I don't have time...but I just do it. Find your preference: do you like one type of exercise or are you prone to flit around from one form to another? Find your type: do you like to do things with purpose or non-purpose when you exercise? Find what you like to do, then gradually change to a more active life just for the fun of it...for the health of it...do it!

3. **Relaxation-Imagery-Meditation (R.I.M.):** This is the most important part of any permanent healing in life. In the silence we see a clearer picture, make better

decisions and get in touch with our body's own Intelligence-Spirit that absolutely knows how to be happy and healthy. Stress is related to all disease. If we are in tune with our body, we can feel what's going on in our body. Take 5 to 30 minutes each day to do nothing physical, just relax and imagine your body being in air, then contemplate nothingness.

4. **Environment:** Be aware of toxic environments — not only household cleaners but places and people can be toxic to wellness. It's the little people standing on our shoulders, the voices of the past that shape our behavior today. Be aware of the household cleaners as well as the person holding the can.

4+1. **Determination:**
Audacity…tenacity…adaptability. These are qualities of centenarians, people who have lived a hundred years or more. It all adds up to *attitude* backed by a belief in something omnipresent. Something all-powerful that we commune with daily but have yet to imagine fully.

The *American Heritage Dictionary* says, "1. Attitude is a position of the body or manner of carrying oneself, indicative of a mood or condition. 2. A state of mind of feeling with regard to a person or thing."

I think it's interesting that the definition of attitude is so closely associated with the position of the body; it indicates an inseparable connection between mind-body-spirit.

Create your journey…

In the following chapters I will share with you what I discovered over the past 11 years that helped me to stay healthy, and follow the real nature of my life's purpose.. The Seven Characters of Life's Theater in Part II created themselves. As I became aware of my negative thoughts and how they ran in my life, I disovered familiar personality traits that gave insight into their effect on health and happiness. Part III, The 3 A's of Healthy, Happy Living, examines the process of Acknowledging the MOT (method of operation thinking) we've used, Accepting the changes necessary and taking Action to alter our perception of the circumstances of our lives. Mini-Bites Insights to a Healthier, Happier You – Part IV is written with common sense, down to earth suggestions for taking charge of your life. Change is an inevitable part of our stay on this planet. Transitional change is made easier by using relaxation-imagery-meditation in Part V to assist the body-mind and spirit in its acceptance.

Attitude

"The longer I live the more I realize the impact of attitude on life. Attitude to me, is more important than facts. It is more important than the past, than education, than money, than circumstances, than failures, than successes, than whatever other people think, say or do. It is more important than appearances, giftedness, or skill. It will make or break a company...a church... a home. The remarkable thing is, we have a choice every day. We cannot change our past. We cannot change the inevitable. The only thing we can do is play on the one string we have, and that is our attitude...I am convinced that life is 10% what happens to me and 90% how I react to it. And so it is with you... we are in charge of our attitudes."

Charles Swindoll

Part II

The Seven Character Roles We Play in Life's Theater

No one knows how long the future will be. We only have today. What would you want your life to look like if today were your only day? Your last day?

Judy Pearson

Let's meet the seven character roles we play in life's theater. I discovered my friends **Gracie Gossip, Ulla Dunnit, Waukeen Wounded, Super Stella, Freda Fine, Nanna Yabut,** and **Nurse Cratchit** as I became aware of my own beliefs and the race consciousness of people around me. (Race consciousness is a set of collective beliefs that are common to all human kind.) I tried to change my beliefs...that didn't work. I tried to avoid them...that didn't work either. One day I decided to embrace them and love the part of me that they responded to, realizing that I had a choice as to how often any of these characters had an active role in my life.

Mission Possible:

Your foot crosses the threshold. You have told yourself that this is going to be a great day. You like the work, the friendly people, and yet for some reason, even when you start out the morning with the idea of having a good day, it fades quickly, like the day you decided to diet. (Wouldn't it be nice if a two-week vacation seemed as long as two weeks of dieting?)

"Good morning," Sally says as you walk through the door. "Good morning. What's new?" is your reply. "Well, what a day! It's already started out bad, and it will probably only get worse. Three people didn't even show up for work today and our filing system is all screwed up." You have just experienced *Mission Possible*. If you choose to accept this assignment, your mission will be to set the tone for the day and not waver from that goal — no matter what happens or what anyone says. Bringing your healthy mind and body to work is literally like opening your lunch box, briefcase, purse, or tool box, and remembering all the characters in your life are there to teach you something. When you learn it, you may notice they no longer play their roles in your life.

How many of these characters do you recognize... in others? ...in yourself?

Gracie Gossip

"Gossip is the art of saying nothing in a way that leaves practically nothing unsaid."

Walter Winchell

"Madeline, Gracie here. I just thought I'd call ya', dear. How are ya'? Are ya' sure? You don't sound fine to me. Oh, me? Getting along. I heard just the other day that Bengie Pawalsky is carrying on with the young blonde lady who wears those tight skimpy outfits two doors down from you. Why, I think she'll catch her death of a cold with those kind of clothes. Oh, I been doin' OK. Just my gallbladder hurt'n.

Yasss, mmmm...Oh, you too, me too. The other day I was in the doctor's office...yasss, just sitting there waiting. I heard the nurse talking about a new disease. Yasss, it hurts all the way from the head to the toes. I think I've got it, you know...yasss, just one thing after another, isn't it. Well, I got to go now. My favorite TV show is on — Ben Casey and Dr. Welby, ya' know. Bye now...

*"Sometimes you can catch disease
by just agreeing with it."*

Judy Pearson

I worked in a wholesale travel agency answering phones and arranging and selling wholesale travel packages to travel agencies. At the end of the day I would leave the office with a headache, my shoulders hiked up around my ears, and wondering why.

I knew this wasn't my life's work, yet I was learning computer skills, clerical skills, people skills...and it paid money. So what was bothering me? I began to pay attention to what my body was hearing while my ears were busy on the phone. In the next cubicle, Gracie had been at her job a long time. She was cheerful and knew everyone who called in by their first name. She sold travel packages, ironing out all the details quickly and smoothly. Subconsciously, my body heard "Hi, Sherri, how are you? What's new with you? Oh, really? Oh, how horrible. What can I do for you today? OK. Sell, sell, sell, sell...Well, you take care now. Oh, you too? Me too? Yes, well that's just awful. That's too bad... Good bye. Click...What a dumb, stupid, woman...She got married to a drunk two months ago and now he's running out on her. It always happens, no matter what you do...oh it's just one thing after another." The next call was the same. Negative messages wrapped in caring words breed confusion, negativity and illness.

Gracie Gossip likes to know the dirt on everyone. The bigger the problem, the better the gossip. She reads the *Inquirer, The Star,* and every rag about everyone because inquiring minds want to know — and Gracie certainly has an inquiring mind concerning other people's business.

I used to listen to friends for hours on the phone tell me about this ailment, their problem child, or their husband who drank too much or didn't come home. I would agree out of courtesy and sympathy. After all, that is the way life is, isn't it? Their stories continued and I continued to listen. I realized, after years of listening and complaining myself, that I was part of the problem, not the solution.

What about this part of us?

Gracie relates best to people who have problems or ailments; she wants to be in the know. Folks have a story to tell and need someone to listen. And they often turn to Gracie. *Ben Casey, Dr. Welby,* and *Dr. Kildare,* live on in her own personal *General Hospital.* Soap operas are her other hobbies and the array of soap opera emotions fill her life. She wants to know what's wrong, not so she can help solve it, but to add your story to her list of what's wrong in the world. Life's a battle. It's just one bad thing after another to overcome.

From my point of view, we have a mind-set on diseases. We believe there is a 3-day flu, a 14-day cold, and 7-year itch. A set-up for failure. Cancer, arthritis, leukemia, multiple sclerosis, AIDS, and others are incurable. Yet people live happy, healthy lives for many years, even after they receive an incurable diagnosis. Did you ever notice that people own their illness by calling it "my cold," "my hay fever," "my cancer," or "my aching back?"

The 3 A's in Part III can help you acknowledge Gracie in yourself and others. Be *willing* to change. Adopt the four letter word *"risk."* Accept and love yourself and others without conditions. You are lovable just the way you are right now. Nothing needs to be added or changed. Act with a new attitude toward life, and life will act with a new attitude toward you!

Ulla Dunnit

"The willingness to accept responsibility for one's own life is the source from which self-respect springs."

Joan Didion

"Elementary, my dear Watson. Elementary. It would not, should not, could not be my fault. Who dunnit? Who dunnit? U dunnit. U dunnit to me...It's not my fault I'm late for work. It's not my fault the car ran out of gas, I had to hitchhike with two gypsies who took me through the desert and over the Rocky Mountains just to get here. I didn't have any choice. It's not my fault.

It's not my fault. U made me do it. U
made me mad. U made me glad. U
made me happy. U made me sad. U
made me sick! U made me well. Oh,
yeah?"

Ulla Dunnit is always pointing her finger at someone else. Who dunnit? Ulla Dunnit, of course. We all
have a little Ulla tucked away, ready to come out when
we don't feel like being responsible for our lives.
Television and radio sing to us, "Blame It On Texas,
Don't Blame It On Me" or "You made me love you, I
didn't want to do it...I didn't want to do it." Did you
do it or did I do it? U dunnit to me.

I was appalled when someone said, "Your thinking
has a direct effect on your health. You are responsible
for your health." Was I responsible for "my cancer?" I
might be responsible for choosing the car in my drive-
way...but cancer?

According the latest research by Dr. Candace Pert,
Ph.D., Rutgers University, "Our bodies are a molecular, psychosomatic communication network." In other
words, every cell in our body has memory and responds to what we feel. Previously it was believed that
endorphins and other chemicals like them which have
a direct effect on our health, were found only in the
brain. Research now indicates they are not only in the
brain but in the immune system, the endocrine system,
and throughout the entire body. The information
network (intelligence) is constantly flowing. These
molecules are being released from one place, diffusing
all over the body, tickling millions of neuropeptides

(receptors) that are on the surface of every cell in our bodies. Everything in our bodies is being run by messenger molecules, many of which are peptides. A peptide is made up of different amino acids. Peptides are amino acids strung together, very much like pearls on a necklace. These peptides are extremely important because they appear to mediate intracellular communication throughout the brain and body. These neuropeptides and their receptors are the biochemical correlates of emotions.

In simple terms, our thoughts are emotions which set off chemical reactions throughout the body at the cellular level and clearly affect our health. We cannot think without feeling, and as we accumulate thoughts they turn into beliefs. Could it be that every time I feel, I record those feelings in my body? Could it be, in simple terms, that after I have recorded enough information about "cancer runs in my family" that I can prove that belief and easily produce cancer in my body? I believe that it is possible to have cancerous thoughts run in a family, as it is possible to have alcoholism, abusive behavior, and other dysfunctions handed down from generation to generation. And the concept of family includes biological family, planetary family, and all other groups in-between.

What about this part of us?
Ulla is the teacher of responsibility. She gave me the opportunity, when I chose to look at myself, to take responsibility for my behavior, even if I felt like blaming my mother, father, brothers, or the teacher who had laid her fingernails into my shoulder over getting

out of line about a piece of paper.

"Is it my fault I'm sick? I feel so guilty. I blame myself for getting cancer. If I hadn't eaten the wrong foods, let others run my life, listened to my hypochondriac mother tell me how cancer and illness were inevitable...If I had only been smart enough to see it coming." I shared this with my counselor. I learned that yes, *I am responsible for my body because of the choices I have made.*

Children Learn What They Live

If a child lives with tolerance,
He learns to be patient.
If a child lives with encouragement,
He learns confidence.
If a child lives with praise,
He learns to appreciate.
If a child lives with fairness,
He learns justice.
If a child lives with security,
He learns to have faith.
If a child lives with approval,
He learns to like himself.
If a child lives with acceptance and friendship,
He learns to find love in the world.
These are the fundamentals to a life well lived.

Anonymous

Waukeen Wounded

"No man can think clearly when his fists are clenched."

George Jean Nathan

"I don't know what's wrong with me. I get a lot of headaches...I'm so tired all the time. Irritable? I think I have a headache right now. Sometimes I feel so weary, it's this piercing pain like having an arrow stuck in my head...The slightest thing sets me off. People say I have a short fuse, or I'm too sensitive. Boy, when you hurt my feelings I don't forget it...I keep a grudge for years, I bury my anger with a big shovel, I stew over hurts, let them eat at me, then when I least expect it...POW! I lose my temper or break into tears. I'm like a hungry cat at Mickey Mouse's birthday party, no mice to eat and I'm supposed to be having fun."

"Don't pay any attention to what I say or do. I don't mean it...I'm just mad. The names I called you?...I don't mean them. What I just did?...I don't mean it either. I don't know what's wrong or right; this is just my way of communicating. I don't mean to cry at the drop of a hat....or...Angry? I feel as though if I really got angry I'd blow apart and be responsible for World War III. I have been so angry so long and hid it so well that I don't know when I am angry."

Waukeen Wounded has an arrow through the head to bring home the point. Are you wondering why you have a headache or are so tense? Think about the time you had a sliver in your foot and no way at the time of getting a pair of tweezers to get it out. By the end of the day your body had tensed up from trying to ignore the pain.

Research indicates that long-term, severe, deep-seated anger, sadness, frustration and self-hatred has an extreme detrimental influence on the immune system. Long-held resentments fester and eat away at the self and ultimately can eat away at the body in the form of tumors, cancer, and other dis-ease. Rage, stuffed because you fear the risk of losing love and approval, breeds dis-ease. If anger has no place to express outwardly it grows and festers inwardly. We give our bodies confusing signals. We tell ourselves, "This time it isn't going to hurt me," yet we feel incapable of doing anything to change the circumstances. Conflicting messages in the body intelligence out even in the cells expresses a tumor, or other dis-ease (against ease) while the rest of the body adapts to the condition.

My mother was insecure all of her life. Her father deserted the family when she was five. My grandmother, with no education, did her best to raise three children by herself. An unstable life of bitterness, anger, and guilt robbed my mother of the kind of LOVE we are suppose to take for granted: the basic foundation we all need — the taken-for-granted LOVE you embody when you are brought up in unconditional love. She was a sweet, loving person when things were going smoothly. When they were not, she became a shoplifter who was seriously ill or abusive, vindictive and cruelly manipulative. My father, a mild-mannered carpenter, was away from home most of the time. He, like most fathers at the time, left the child-raising to the wife and mother. Mom guarded her sanity in his presence. She didn't want to burden him with her hurts. I grew up confused. I never knew what mom was going to do when I came through the door from school. I could be greeted by, "Hi, honey how was your day?" or "Who the hell do you think you are, some kind of queen or something? You no-good slob, get in there and clean up your room." I knew that if I expressed my anger and frustration, I would get the back of her hand, if not worse. I did my best to be a good girl and survive.

This is not about blaming mother. She did what she had been taught to do and what she believed she was supposed to do. She was a very frustrated and angry child herself. These misunderstood feelings and dysfunctional family survival tactics were handed down to me and my brothers as if they were the instructions for the care and preservation of the family quilt and heirlooms. Life seemed to be a place where people hurt each other and weren't allowed to tell of their hurt. A place where love was not to be trusted, for in a fleeting moment, for it may turn to rage.

What about this part of us?

"Sometimes she scolded herself so severely as to bring tears into her eyes."

Alice in Wonderland

You don't have to scold yourself — or bring tears to your eyes. Healing is about loving, accepting and forgiving. And the only place to begin is with yourself.

Super Stella

"Life is entirely too time-consuming."

Irene Peter

"Let's see now...not to worry; if I make a list I won't forget. Right? Get the kids off to school by 7 am, throw a load into the washer (whites with softener, no bleach). Pick up the magazines, clothes and dirt before they hit the living room floor. Do I have enough food for 15 for dinner tonight? I hope they like artichokes. Oh yes, it's off to work...Harry said that project is due in on Monday. Hurry, hurry...Groceries, I don't know what to get, maybe no one likes artichokes...then pick up Suzy at ballet. I wish I could have watched her perform. And Ron says he's really good at baseball. Oh, well, Ed will need his suit from the cleaners..."

"Super Stella, cook, maid, chauffeur, and mind reader, ssheeeesshh!!!! The race is on — did I forget anything? My heart is pounding. Are we having fun yet?"

This is grade A, number 1, blue ribbon stress. Run, run all day, then collapse on the couch unable to think, read, or carry on a conversation. I think I accomplished something, but what was it again?

That was stress and this is stress.
It's your white-knuckle grip and a balloon filled with air that keeps you just inches from the deadly current of the Colorado River. White water peppers your face as your mosquito-riddled arms regain their hold. Get ready, another jolt. Now airborne, will the raft head into the rocks, crash, and spill its occupants, or steer steady to the center flow of the river? This is Stress. Your heart is pounding. Are you having fun yet?

It is estimated that 85% or more of all medical complaints are stress related. The more obvious of these complaints are headaches, ulcers, insomnia, indigestion, and high blood pressure. Some of the lesser known ailments are sexual dysfunction, diarrhea, muscle aches, heart attack, seizures, chronic illness (flu, colds), grinding of teeth, exhaustion, and cancer. The first stress, grade A number 1 seems endless. Never-ending daily routine, running the gambit of emotions, worry, anger, fear, or guilt with every thought. In the second stress, your white knuckle raft ride, you have no time to worry about the kids, the office, the dinner party, or how you measure up as a human being. You are living and enjoying the moment (if raft riding is fun for you).

What about this part of us?

A human being's natural state is to be in the ebb and flow of life, like the river with its ups, downs, turns, twists, highs and lows. Stress of life can give you the vital energy of life or it can drain the very life out of you. Stress is not simply nervous tension, something to be avoided, or something unpleasant. Damaging stress is an attitude, based on belief. When you were a kid you had chores you liked doing and others, as my mom would say, were like "pulling eye teeth to get you to do." Thank God she never tried to actually pull them. Stress can motivate us, encourage us to keep going when life gets complicated or difficult. It spurs us into action in the midst of crisis and makes life exciting.

Emotion is the connection of mind and body. Everything we think, we feel; everything we feel is stored in the memory in our body's cells. When we choose an emotion, the body cells react from memory. We may be a victim of an injustice, or the recipient of the greatest party on earth. No matter what the age or circumstances, we know what we feel. We may think we have forgotten but it is stored in every cell. The good news is, we have a choice. When we are aware of our Stella, Ulla, Waukeen, Nanna, Gracie, Freda, or Nurse Cratchit we can take charge of the emotion. We can change the outcome by changing our belief about the experience.

We can choose fear, anger, worry, guilt and victimhood as life's stimuli. Learning to put these potentially dangerous emotions into balance creates joy, peace and harmony in the body and mind.

Stress is the fastest growing dis-ease in the western world because few people know how to deal with their stresses and adapt to their ever-changing environment. And few people are willing to change their responses to life's events.

Dr. Candace Pert, Ph.D., Visiting Professor at the Center for Molecular and Behavioral Neuroscience, Rutgers University, and a consultant in peptide research in Rockville, Maryland says, "That's what's so interesting about emotions. They're the bridge between the mental and the physical, or the physical and the mental. It's either way."

Whether you ride in the front, side or back of the raft, at home, office, or play, your experience is a matter of choice. As in the raft ride, you cannot simply sit and do nothing. You must form a partnership with others for safe passage. When we cooperate as a team, we directly affect the quality and substance of everyone's ride — of everyone's life.

Freda Fine

*"It's better to be a lion for a day than
a sheep all your life."*

Sister Elizabeth Kenny

"Oh, I'm fine. My thumb? Oh, I
smashed it in a car door...but it's fine.
I went to the grocery store yesterday.
Well, the automatic door swung open,
hit my nose and blackened my eyes,
but I'm fine. I got my cart, caught my
heel on a can of green beans, and doing
the splits, I cleared the frozen food
section in 10 seconds flat. I'm still picking the peas out of my hair...but I'm
just fine. Nothing ever upsets me. I

won't let it. It's true my husband left for the Bahamas with his secretary. Just before he left he totaled my car. I'm fine. The kids are dope addicts. My 15-year-old daughter is pregnant. I'm fine. Mother just told me she is divorcing my father, but everything is just fine."

When I was growing up, my survival tactic had always been to keep the peace, keep life on an even keel. I learned that it was better to say "fine" than to explain even the simplest of things to my emotionally unstable mother. I told myself that if I could control it by denying the problems, everything would be just fine. Most of us have been **Freda Fine** at one time or another. We often see her in others before we see her in ourselves. News flash! If you can see Freda clearly in others, Freda lives in you.

I exercised everyday, changed my diet, and yet my health worsened. My large-framed 5' 9" body carried 120 pounds like a bag of bones. Friends couldn't convince me there was something wrong, even though the telltale signs of gray pale skin were evident. I was wearing the results of a year of denial, keeping my emotions under wraps, maintaining a stiff upper lip and all that. If someone asked me how I was I always answered, *"I'm fine."*

While my attitude about the medical profession hardened, I was far from what Dr. Bernie Siegel calls the *exceptional patient.* I didn't know how to say, "This is what I want from a doctor and/or treatment." I simply wasn't strong enough to become an "exceptional patient" within the medical system.

What about this part of us?

We are always faced with problems and situations. That's a fact. If we deny our feelings, we resent. Deep-seated grief begins. As we give up our rights, life begins to eat away at the self. A cycle of not liking the self and not being willing to say so can lead to serious dis-ease.

We can choose our feelings, own up to our feelings, or we can live in a state of sugar-coating, rose-colored glasses and hope we never have to deal with life. When we face our fears, we are saying we are worth whatever it takes to be happy and healthy every day. We each deserve the best in life every moment. *You are great, stupendous, voluptuous, stunning, beautiful, gorgeous, excellent, intelligent, creative, whole, happy, or tired, lonely, venerable, sad, mad...but never "fine."*

"A lot of people die at 40, but they aren't buried until 30 years later."

General George S. Patton

Nanna Yabut

"We cannot escape the fact that at every step of life is a significant choice. We choose, and the mind creates. We should endeavor to choose that which will express always a greater life, and we must remember that the Spirit is always seeking to express love and beauty."

Ernest Holmes

"**Nanna Yabut**, I would exercise .. **Nanna Yabut**, I can't because I'm too out of shape. **Nanna Yabut**, my hair might get messed up. **Nanna Yabut**, I don't have time. **Nanna Yabut**, what if I pull a muscle? **Nanna Yabut**, I only have so many heartbeats left, and don't want to waste them."

Nanna Yabut sets limits, then lives within them. Nanna answered for me most of the time when it came to changing my thinking. My limits were my fears — and fear almost killed me.

I spent a year denying cancer, surgery, or the stress I was under. I told myself *yabut* the hysterectomy, yabut the tumor the size of a grapefruit is gone. I don't have cancer any more. And yet I didn't believe it. I filtered out what I didn't want to hear. Selective hearing almost cost me my life. You see, I thought positive thinking, diet and exercise was all I needed to get well. Never mind the old cancerous thoughts that had gotten me here. Fear ran my life. I would have gone to the doctor yabut what if he says "chemotherapy" again? Yabut I was stubborn and contrary. I had always gone against authority. Yabut I had never bet my life on it. Yabut hesitation slowed down the supply of good flowing though my life.

The fear of dying and the fear of not knowing whether I could stick with the lifestyle changes consumed my thoughts. I had read that your mind can change your body. But how do I get past the fear?

I was afraid of what other people might do, say or think. I compromised for peace, because, "Yabut, they won't love me any more." I wanted to try a vegetarian diet, yabut Ed's a meat-and-potatoes man and our two (junk food) teenagers, what will they think? Yabut if you don't take chemotherapy, are you going to die? Going against the way life had always been was a tough decision. We have always eaten this way...so what? They say chemotherapy is the only answer...so what? I could weigh the consequences of my actions and yabut myself out of doing anything. Facing my mortality quickened my decisions. I remembered my father's words "Yabuts don't get anywhere, they are like the jack rabbits on these 40 acres, moving fast, jumping high with no place to go."

What about this part of us?
I once heard a quote: "Best is the enemy of better." Think about it. If you can't be the best, why try — right? Wrong! Just do it!

Yabuts can make the difference in recovery. Yabuts create limitations in our lives and in our health. A study of 100 tuberculous patients revealed that those who were emotionally disturbed (worries of home and family) had a swifter form of the disease than those free from strain. Other studies have shown that in many cases of diabetes, patients have suffered from severe emotional shock; that arthritic attacks frequently run parallel to acute mental upsets; that worry can accelerate tooth decay; that cancer is triggered by emotional shock or upheaval approximately two years or more before it takes form in the body. Science is continually finding more evidence of the mind-body-spirit connection.

If we put limits on what we can achieve, the Universal Law of Cause and Effect says, "Yes, you are right." No matter what we think, what we believe, we get to be right. Becoming constantly aware of and responsible for our thoughts puts the yabuts right in our face. You can choose to listen to them and let their limitations dictate your life or you can go beyond "the way life has always been" to unlimited possibilities.

Nurse Cratchit

"Striving for excellence motivates you: striving for perfection is demoralizing."

Harriet Braiker

"Must I explain this again?! We will take our medicine at 1:00 pm on the dot. We will follow the rules and instructions. We do know the rules, don't we? We know the directions? If you do not understand the instructions, I will repeat them until you do. We will stay within the lines. Speak when we are spoken to and dot our i's and cross our t's. We will not say or do anything to disturb others. We will do things properly or not at all. We must be an accurate, in-control, rigid, stuffed-shirt, tight-assed role model. There is only one way of doing it, and that is my way. If you don't do it my way `we must not be communicating'."

I worked with a "Nurse Cratchit" called Hilda. She wanted everything done her way and reminded me of Nurse Ratchet in the movie "One Flew Over The Cuckoo's Nest." Hilda was young, a recent college graduate and a supervisor in her father's business of camera-ready advertising ads. The pressure of having to be it all and know it all was incredible. She was critical and resented anyone who might know more than she did. She put up a good front but inside was desperately seeking love and approval.

Hilda had to know it all, perform it all, and be it all, better than everyone in the plant. Hilda and I spent a year working around each other. (I do mean around!) My job was to lay out photographs for a publication, making sure they were straight, captioned correctly, and met the overall publication specifications. Perched near my desk for the better part of the year, Hilda the vulture kept a critical, silent vigil over everything I did, repeating instructions, explaining how, "We must not be communicating," if anything wasn't to her liking. As simple as my job was and as many times as I had done it, I never could please her. No matter how great the job, when it was done it got a "Ho-hum" response.

All I wanted was to do my job the best I knew how. To Hilda's credit, she was an equal opportunity supervisor: everyone got the same Nurse Cratchit treatment. But no one said anything.

One Monday morning my desk held the final straw. Large sticker notes in red ink instructed me to take this project completely apart and start over because it was not satisfactory. Hilda seemed to know I wasn't a follower, and she needed followers, often at the expense of the company's time and money. Her way was the only way. When I told Hilda's father that I wasn't willing to work under these conditions, he was astonished. He had no idea there were any problems with the employees. He didn't want to know, either.

My story of Hilda illustrates an outside example of Nurse Cratchit stress. But there are also the critical stories we carry around in our heads that keep us from moving forward. I was sure I couldn't use a typewriter. When someone asked, "Can you type?" I cringed, and my shoulders went rigid. I can still remember typing class, three sentence papers, graded D for effort and Mrs. Sesely's head shaking from side to side. "You will never be good at much if you can't type." When we believe in past comments, we limit our future

When we get caught up in the expectations of others, we become a person looking for love in the deeds he or she does. I could see Hilda in myself and how I had tried to be a perfect little girl, accurate and right all the time. I began to acknowledge and be aware of my actions and thoughts. Then I could forgive others who used Nurse Cratchit to rule their world.

What about this part of us?
We need to teach our kids that they are good

enough, no matter what. Schools today validate the student for following the rules, coloring within the lines of a system created in the 1890's. Our world is changing. Our school systems, health care systems, and our family systems are being forced to take on preventive practices in order to serve each other.

Education is the only preventive practice. If education were our first priority, our children and ourselves would come first, before new prison costs, before war defense costs, before new hospitals. Children would be supported in learning about their bodies, their minds and especially their spirit. Our top concern for all peoples would be that basic needs for spiritual, mental, and physical growth through education (preventive health-enriching practices) would be an everyday occurrence. Instead we teach generations to strive toward an unattainable goal. "If I could do one more thing, get one more degree, win one more award, then I would win the love I need and want." We are all looking for LOVE. Always trying to be a perfect little daughter or a great and wonderful son in order to be loved and feel lovable.

How does this striving influence dis-ease? Feeling unloved and criticized creates resentments. Research has shown that a personality (or role) such as Nurse Cratchit increases our stress level so dis-eases such as high blood pressure, arthritis, hypertension, and cancer can overcome our immune system and make a home in us.

Using the cycling process of the 3 A's of Healing can assist you in making healthy changes permanently.

Part III

If you can see it in your mind,
It can come true,
If you can feel it in your heart,
It can be for you.
If you can conceive it,
If you can believe it.
Then there isn't any reason
That you can't achieve it.
If you can picture in your head
Your dearest dream,
There's nothing in the world
That's too extreme—
For you to be, for you to do,
For you to have — it waits for you
If you can see it in your mind.

Jean Anderson

The 3 A's of Healthy, Happy Living

Acknowledge Love

"You can only learn to love by loving."

Iris Murdock

Wouldn't you agree that you can't overcome something unless you first acknowledge its presence? The *American Heritage Dictionary* defines acknowledge as: "To admit the validity, authority, or truth of."

I spent a year denying I had cancer, the need for an operation, or that the whole crisis had happened. I told myself that with the hysterectomy done and the grapefruit-sized tumor removed, I didn't have cancer any more. The doctor's insistence that there were still cancer cells floating around, and that chemotherapy was the only cure, added to my depression. I didn't believe it, yet all the world around me did. You see, I figured that if I had only positive thoughts, I could get well on my own. Yet fear ran my life. I am a stubborn, contrary person who has always gone against authority. That's probably why my mother and I didn't get along very well. She conformed to it, I fought it. Denial creates an unhealthy way to confront fear. It freezes the decision-making process.

With instructions not to lift, drive a car, or do much of anything, recovery from the 6 inch incision drove me crazy. I have never been good at doing nothing. The months it took to get back into the swing of life, plus the fear of dying and the fear of not knowing whether I could stick with the lifestyle changes I had set up for myself, consumed my thoughts. I had read that your mind can change your body. I thought that all I had to do was deny the existence of disease and it would be gone. I was scared to trust myself or anyone, especially doctors.

I exercised and changed my diet, yet my health worsened. I still looked like a bag of bones with pale grey skin. Since my attitude toward the medical profession had hardened, I wasn't strong enough to become an "exceptional patient" within the medical system. It wasn't until I let go of my fear, anchored myself spiritually, acknowledged my condition, and faced the fact that my thoughts had created my cancer, now I could choose new thoughts and create life differently — the way I wanted it. Whatever that looked like.

When we understand and acknowledge that LOVE is the nature of our spirit and the spirit of others, we realize that all we want is an opportunity to be LOVED and to LOVE.

Accept Love

*"When it comes right down to it,
the secret of having it all is loving it all."*

Dr. Joyce Brothers

Accepting has to happen on the inside of you.
There was only one way for me to make permanent
changes to a lifestyle that had been running on empty,
in a cancerous mode, for 40 years. I needed to go
within, to penetrate my conscious belief system, and
learn to accept new ideas about the way I perceived
life.

I began by getting relaxation tapes with messages
that allowed me to get in touch with my mind and
body, which allowed the Spirit in me to take over and
create well-ness.

I soon realized that R.I.M. (Relaxation-Imagery-
Meditation) could help me to work out anything —
from relationship situations and money issues to my
life's purpose.

It was not always easy to sit in the silence and let
go of my ego ideas. No matter how a certain person
may be acting toward me (or, rather, my perception of
their behavior), my job was to clear my thoughts and
realize that there was nothing I could do to change
anyone else. I learned that forgiveness was the biggest

barrier and biggest breakthrough to turning life from drudgery to freedom. In order to have what you seek, you must learn the art of adaptable forgiveness. Life is the continual practice of forgiveness. I will never forget one client's words. "When I do my meditation I send my spirit out to the people I may have offended that day." There will always be someone or something to forgive. Accept everything as a force always moving toward the good, knowing that there really is no bad guy or good guy, only God guys.

Act in Love

AªA

> *"Loving is not just caring deeply;*
> *it's, above all, understanding."*

Francoise Sagan

Act in Love. Being kind to yourself ensures you will be kind to others.

What is this invisible thing called the power of LOVE? It's elusive. We can see it in a smile. We can hear it in a loved one's voice. We can't live without it. We know it exists, yet if we were to order a pound of LOVE we wouldn't be able to put a price on it or measure it. The attitude of LOVE is the glue that holds us all together. Without LOVE we wither and die.

If we wither and die without love's influence, is love giving us life? Why would we want to misuse and deplete this power by hating or grudging? Why would we as humans think we can live without opening to a power that increases our potential unlimitedly?

> *"The limits of the possible extend infinitely*
> *beyond impossibility."*

Anonymous

As it is with all 3 A's— acknowledging, accepting, acting—it is a constant cycle of reconditioning your life. There is no end to acknowledging where you are, accepting new things internally, or acting with love.

Here are some of the things you can do to bring more Love into your life.

- **The Act of Love** starts by giving. Giving unconditionally, without thought of return, to everyone, excluding no one.

- **The Act of Love** happens when you love yourself 100%, 100% of the time. Giving yourself hugs, rewards, and honor sets the stage for even more success reflecting and unfolding in your life. As you accept yourself as lovable just the way you are right now, you can accept others just the way they are.

- **The Act of Love** means realizing that love is a living breathing force, an object, something that can be used to bring peace to any situation.

- **The Act of Love** is learning to take responsibility for the creation of the world and your corner of the world via the power of your thoughts.

- **The Act of Love** is living life as if you are on a perpetual peace mission. Every morning just after you awaken, stay in the silence for 5-30 minutes remembering your connection with your creator and remembering your purpose on this planet is **The Act of Love.**

This coupon is good for

whatever your heart desires,

whenever you are ready

to accept your good!

SIGNED: The Universe

Acknowledge: the good in EVERY situation.

Accept: your own greatness.

Act: as if it were already done.

The 3 A's for Gracie Gossip

Acknowledge Gracie as part of what you see, hear, say, and do in life. Learning a new behavior, a new lifestyle is not always synonymous with fast and easy, but the time spent is worth every minute of saying an affirmation over and over again; or listening to people joke about how you keep repeating yourself; or people teasing you about your diet, foo-fooing exercise, scoffing at meditation. It's worth it to live the rest of your life (however long that is) in quality. Acknowledge what you want to change and keep focused on your goal.

Accept new attitudes and beliefs by repeating affirmations during the day. As a break, once a day find a place to practice R.I.M. (Relaxation-Imagery-Meditation).

If we hear a thought said often enough it becomes a belief. Judge Thomas Troward, a great philosopher, talked about grooves of thoughts in the physiology of the brain that holds memory. Enough negative thoughts collectively create negative grooves. By repeating positive, counter affirmations you can physically change the size of the grooves. When I changed my listening and response habits, some of my friends changed too — some left my life, while others changed their conversation styles with me. Accept yourself and the changes in your life that happen as a result of your new attitude.

Act consciously with love. How do we face the

world of Gracies? Become aware of them. Soap operas, gossip rags, hemorrhoids, mouthwashes, antacids, toothpaste, pain relievers, and cold remedies are clues to her presence. After listening to an actress or actor suffering with a snotty rag in hand, if you don't have one or more of these ailments...you soon could have. Act consciously by talking the talk and walking the walk of a healthy, happy life.

3 Ways to Filter Out Toxic Mind Talk:

1. Watch television news only once a week. You will catch up easily, everything is repeated 10 times anyway. When you're through, send your spirit of goodwill to all mentioned.

2. Use the remote control mute though the violence and commercials. Go for a walk when soap operas are on the air.

3. Gravitate to humorous shows and movies and keep it light-hearted. Laughter from within endures. As Norman Cousins says in his book *Anatomy of an Illness*, "I was greatly elated by the discovery that there is a physiologic basis for the ancient theory that laughter is good medicine."

The 3 A's for Ulla Dunnit

Acknowledge your responsibility for what you are experiencing. Now ask yourself, "If I could change this experience in my future, what would I have it look like?"

The truth is, no one can make you feel bad. No one can make you feel glad. No one can make you feel anything. We have total choice every minute on how we feel. It's the only thing we do have choice about. It's the only thing we need have choice about. So the phrases, "You made me mad…you make me sick…," just don't cut it. It's not true. I caught myself saying these phrases all the time. I could have been saying, "I feel bad, sad, or glad…" But I wasn't accepting responsibility for my feelings.

You no longer have to take responsibility for others' feelings and problems. Nor can you blame others for your feelings and problems. Allow a place for the healing of the situation to begin. When we point the finger of accusation, we are really pointing to ourselves because as you point at others, three of your fingers point back at you. Try it.

Accept the loving responsibility of your life by loving yourself. Choosing, correcting, and forgiving yourself changes your belief system. Learn to be easy on yourself. Let go of the past, practice daily the art of forgiveness. Forgive yourself. Make amends with others who you feel have wronged you. La Rouchefaucould said, "One forgives to the degree that one loves." Every time we feel, we record our feelings in our body. Those feelings are recorded on the cellular level. If we do not forgive, accept, and love, we keep these old feelings in the body, where they can harbor dis-ease.

Act by taking charge...taking responsibility is being aware of your self, your thoughts, and your actions. Listen to your words, thoughts, and beliefs. Be aware of shifting the blame to others. This may seem to allow you to think you are right and/or save face. The only way you can truly begin to improve your health or solve a problem is to own your actions, the ones that got you where you are today. Low self-esteem leads to neglect and ignorance, and allows you to play the victim role. This creates dis-ease. Allow yourself and others the quality of being a healthy, happy human. Realize you are in control of the world you create.

"Our thought, being an activity of the One Mind within us, provides a pathway for the flow of the cease-less creative action of Law bringing into our experience a tangible manifestation of our thought."

Ernest Holmes, *The Magic of the Mind*

The 3 A's for Waukeen Wounded

Acknowledge The biggest breakthrough in my healing came when I began to forgive myself and love myself enough to forgive others. Why me, why forgive? I was the one who had been wronged. Okay. I figured I had been the victim here. Forgive everyone in my life who had ever done me wrong? Talk about taking on the world!

What I learned was to forgive myself first. I had been hard on myself for not having the guts to speak up. Gobs of *"if onlys"* were in my thoughts. *If only* I had done this. *If only* I had been enough. I needed to forgive my parents, teachers, doctors, lawyers and candlestick makers, if need be. One of my counselors suggested drawing pictures of my anger, naming the person or circumstance, and then burning it in my fireplace. I knew I would never forget what horrible things that had happened to me, but I could let go of the feelings I associated with those things. Forgiveness played the biggest role in my recovery. It felt good letting go of the beliefs and feelings that were keeping me in a state of cancer, a state of dis-ease.

Forgiveness is a life-giving process. The man who molested me when I was two years old, the grandfather who deserted his family and never got to know his beautiful children and grandchildren— as those feelings of memory came to the surface of my conscious mind, I learned to forgive one more time, time and time again.

Accept I know a woman who has cancer flare-ups every few years. Divorced 19 years, she still carries the wounds of an unhealed relationship. She is happily remarried. Yet anger and resentment rule the conversation. Dealing with the past can bring up painful memories that get in the way of one's happiness. Healthy relationships happen when people learn to look *past* the past and deal with each other in the moment. That in-the-moment feeling can only be accomplished by forgiveness. I have found that until we forgive (which doesn't mean "forget") we carry anger, hate and frustration as potential dis-eases. **Accept** that from now on you will practice the rewarding, healthy art of forgiving. Commit to resolve the hurts from your past. Live life in the present moment. The past is gone; there is nothing you can do to change it. If we let our past beliefs and thoughts run our lives, our health will reflect the results. Imagine that hurt, anger and frustration have left their memory in every cell of your body. Let's learn the practice of releasing these now. Practice meditating daily to deepen your awareness of yourself. Use **"The Meditation for the Stressful Times of Forgiveness"** in Part V to practice the process of forgiveness leading to a healthy mind and a healthy body.

Act with the action of adaptable forgiveness.

Centurions (people who live to be a hundred years old or more), evaluated in a recent study were found to be four predominant types:

1. A Positive Person. Their attitude is always to look at the glass as half full and believe that it is enough. They like themselves just the way they are in

this lifetime, right now.

2. A Committed Person. They are committed to a purpose that gives them satisfaction and a feeling of completeness.

3. An Active Person. Physically active walking, running, gardening, trying new activities.

4. An Adaptable Person. They adapt and choose their surroundings wisely. They cope with losses and disappointments of friends and loved ones as part of everyday life.

"Experience is not what happens to you: it is what you do with what happens to you."

Aldous Huxley

The 3 A's for Nurse Cratchit

Acknowledge the Nurse Cratchit in yourself as well as anyone else who plays the game of perfection. Acknowledge that we are individuals who come from different walks of life. Listen to your critical voices and become aware of how often you use Nurse Cratchit to make yourself right or others wrong. Be aware of your body and how it feels. Never be afraid to be wrong or bend with the current of life's river. Flexibility and openness to mistakes is a healthy virtue. Stay firmly centered in positive thoughts and let go of rigidity.

Accept Nurse Cratchit as a friend who keeps track of the P's and Q's. In your meditation time send Nurse Cratchit lots of love and let it be all right for her acting through you to be who she is. When we are less afraid of making mistakes we are more creative. Allow yourself to receive and give Love from others even if you're not always perfect. Let go of the pressure and stress of having to be perfect.

Act and know you are capable and deserving. Here are suggestion for letting go of Nurse Cratchit:

1. Constantly practice finding ways to love yourself unconditionally.

2. Laugh at your mistakes, even the ones that seem so serious. Life is too short to hold on to old criticisms of yourself and others.

3. Count your mistakes as accomplishments, knowing that you are doing life to the best of your ability and are always subject to change.

The 3 A's for Super Stella

Acknowledge how your body feels. Do you know who you are? Do you know what stresses you? Look at your day. Are you on the couch by 8:00 pm, unable to carry on more than a three-word conversation? "Yes, I did." " No, I don't." "Maybe tomorrow…" When we pull away from the nature of ourselves, our senses dull, our memories become foggy, thus crippling our thinking and weakening our body. It reduces efficiency and productivity and stirs up negative emotions. What is Stella saying to you? Is it time to stop and smell the rhubarb?

Accept the changes in your harried life. One step at a time, you can become aware of, and make friends with, Stella. She provides you with life-giving energy as you learn to use stress to complement your life and not short-circuit the battery. Relax and calm your body. Focus your imagery on letting go of thoughts for 5 to 30 minutes a day. Yes, I am the expert at excuses for not taking time for me in a quiet place. The rewards (after fighting the practice) are well worth it. I think more clearly, get more done, feel better physically, and I think I even have fewer wrinkles on my skin!

Act within the nature of you. The nature of all humans is to be on planet earth in balance with all things around us. Take relaxation exercises with you into your day, by practicing R.I.M. Recognize good, bad, and ugly stress. **Good stress:** you feel great about it when it's over. **Bad stress:** you feel unfulfilled when it's over. **Ugly stress:** manifests in the form of headaches, tumors, arthritis, diabetes, etc. Stress comes into our lives, puts pressure on our bodies and minds, and asks us to adapt and to adjust.

If we are not willing to slow down and take care, our body's own intelligence-spirit will do it for us. It will slow us down and force us to get the rest and quiet that our body-mind needs.

Four potentially stressful areas of our lives:

Beginnings: birth, marriage, pregnancy, gain of a family member, marital reconciliation.

Family: health, in-laws, spouse starts or stops working, new living conditions, new mortgage, son or daughter leaves home.

Work: change in responsibilities, different line of work, business readjustment, financial state change, outstanding personal achievement.

Endings: death, divorce, separation, retirement, change of employment.

You cannot escape change, but you can lessen its effect on the body and mind by getting to know yourself and loving who you are. Healing is simple, but not necessarily easy. Healing is practice, persistence, and perseverance, leading to presence and peace.

The 3 A's for Freda Fine

Acknowledge Freda in yourself and others. Acknowledge what you hear, say and feel when Freda is around you. Listen for the answer to the simple question, "How are you feeling?" Then answer truthfully.

Accept and love Freda for all the lessons you have learned and will continue to learn. In the silence of your thoughts look at your life as a life filled with different opportunities and circumstances. Give yourself permission to feel the anger, disappointment, fear, guilt, or worry. Let Freda know that she is secure in your life, that she no longer has to live behind the thin veil of denial. The use of meditation can quicken your path to appreciating yourself and loving the Freda in you and others.

Act by telling yourself that you are "not fine anymore." Put your shoulders back, head up, and walk proud that no matter what happens, no matter how many mistakes you make, you are still extremely and exceptionally lovable. How are you? You are everything great, stupendous, voluptuous, stunning, beautiful, gorgeous, excellent, intelligent, creative, whole, happy, or tired, lonely, venerable, sad, mad, but never "fine."

The 3 A's for Nanna Yabut

Acknowledge what you like and dislike and what you want to change about your yabuts. Ready to exercise? *"Yabut* what if I pull a muscle?" Be kind to yourself (no guilt needed here) and say to yourself... "Yes, but if I never try, I will never know." Now choose your story. Do you like the fact you may never exercise? Do you like the limits it puts on you? Sure, we all make excuses, but what do you now choose? It's okay if it's not what you chose in the past. This is a new moment, a new opportunity for choice.

Accept what you can and cannot change. Accept what you can change inch by inch, day by day. Grow a bigger space in your life for healthy changes. Meditate daily, focusing on the image of the way you would like life to be. Your mind and body will store the information *as a belief*, and accept the energy and vitality that makes you feel better. Accept what you cannot change. You are probably not a clone of Raquel Welch, or any other muscled body-builder. You are you, a loving child of God learning to love yourself just the way you are right now, accepting change as a friend.

Act is taking action — ain't no way around it. Act from your center of balance and peace of mind. Do you want to change your exercise habits? Decide to exercise. Make it social and fun. Pay the price it takes to be committed. Brainstorm first, considering cost, distance, and child care so you will have most of your excuses out of the way. I know a friend who decides to exercise every year or so. She makes it a big production, at the track everyday 5:30 AM for 2 hours. That lasts about a week and then it's back to nothing. Listen to your body; it knows what it needs to feel healthy. Listen to the signals of how you feel when you hear "yabut" come out of your mouth or invade your thoughts. Be kind and patient with yourself. It took years to get where you are, and you have learned a lot along the way. The yabuts have served you well until now, so let them be your friend.

Exercise is just one example of how we use Nanna Yabut to keep us from optimum health and happiness. We all have a little Nanna popping up now and then.

So Nanna, my dear, how would you like a nice desk job? Somewhere where you can give advice, yet won't run the show and be able to say, "yabut, think before you leap...yabut, why am I doing this? Is it fun? Does it challenge me?" Yabut, does it matter what others think? Nanna and I used to fight over who was going to wear the hat at our house. Now we are friends. I have learned to look at my beliefs in limitations as life's small hurdles and realize that limitations only exist in my thoughts and not in Universal Spirit. As I practice meditation I literally bring my fears to the altar of spiritual peace and balance, I can look at Nanna Yabut as a friend and work with this character to safeguard me when I need it and know when I am limiting myself.

Part IV

Mini-bite Insights to a Healthier You

"The true way to render ourselves happy is to love our duty and find in it our pleasure."

Francoise de Motteville

These mini-bite insights are designed to assist you with the "how to's" of accepting more wellness and happiness in your life.

I have received many books from my friends. When I was depressed, upset and confused, I couldn't begin to read them. It felt overwhelming to take on an entire book. These mini-bite insights are short and easy to read for those of you who may be dealing with the challenge of dis-ease in your lives. We are here to share with each other, so please give this book to others facing a challenge of any sort. If I can do it, anyone can — I do mean anyone. If you are willing to create life living in the moment and being happy, then **Cleaning The Closet, Ledge Living, Counting Awes, Push-it, Baby, Push-it, Devoted Eating, High Hopes, Laugh at Yourself,** and **Trying on a Coat** will assist you in your journey of healthy change. Enjoy!

Resolutions

People are unreasonable, illogical, and self-centered.
Love them anyway.

If you do good, people may accuse you of selfish
motives. **Do good anyway.**

If you are successful, you may win false friends and
true enemies. **Succeed anyway.**

The good you do today may be forgotten tomorrow.
Do good anyway.

Honesty and transparency make you vulnerable.
Be honest anyway.

What you spend in years building may be destroyed
overnight. **Build anyway.**

People who really want help may attack you if
you help them. **Help them anyway.**

Give the world the best you have and you may get hurt.
Give the world your best anyway.

The world is full of conflict.
Choose peace of mind anyway.

Anonymous

Cleaning the Closet

"You don't get to choose how you're going to die. Or when. You can decide how you're going to live."

Joan Baez

Cleaning the closet is an exercise in being intensely aware of your thoughts all day, every moment. A tall order, I know. Become totally aware of every thought you have for one entire day. It's a lesson in how to laugh at yourself and notice what you are saying to your body, mind and life. When you take time to focus your thoughts, you can stay in constant touch with your intuition. The feeling part of us than automatically knows how to bring good into our lives. It reminds me of the young man studying with a famous guru. He asked his master, "Master, what is the meaning of life?" The master replied, "The answer is in the lotus leaf. If you gaze into it and upon it long enough you will know the meaning of life." The master was asking only for the student to focus.

Our mind is like a closet. All right, so your mind is more than that. Imagine a dark hole which gets stuffed with thoughts, both good and bad, all day...stuffed until the thoughts keep the door from closing. Our bodies react in much the same way as the closet. When it believes enough of the negative thoughts we feed it from television, radio, media, mom, dad, teachers, doctors, lawyers, etc., it shows up on the body in one form or another. My wake up call happened when my

86   HEALTHY MIND, HEALTHY BODY

body said, "I've had enough contradictory information. You say you want to be happy but you do nothing to let that happen. You really believe in cancer, so..."

Cancer is a fact of life, bound to happen, or so I thought. My mom's struggle with illness all her life contributed to this perception. She was in and out of the hospitals for nervous breakdowns, tumors, polio, lockjaw, and cancer. As a child I thought she was faking illness to get a rest (which she may have been). I resented her because it seemed that as soon as she had had enough rest she was home and everything was back to normal. "That's how life is going to be for me — a struggle," I thought.

Nature did not put up a wall between mind and body. We did. Or think we did. Our own boundaries to wellness are only limited by beliefs. Beliefs are thoughts we have conditioned ourselves to believe in. Some are good for our bodies and others are not. The more we live from the nature of our spirit, understanding the nature of uniqueness and sameness, the greater health and happiness we can achieve.

Thoughts (the thing we walk around creating every minute of every day) hooking up with emotions, desires, and beliefs about self image, our body, food, health, exercise, relationships, careers, and even life purpose determine our susceptibility to dis-eases such as cancer, heart disease, arthritis, and diabetes. Are you willing to change the contents of your closet (your present collection of thoughts)? That's how healing is done. It's not always easy; it's a life long exercise, and it is worth every minute.

Take a few minutes to answer these questions:

A. Are you willing to let go of the thoughts that created your illness experience? Are you willing to be understanding and forgiving of yourself for having believed them?

B. Are you willing to become aware of the body's intelligence, begin to talk to it with kindness and listen to its answers?

C. What are you willing to give up? Some of the things you have attracted into your life are not healthy for you. Finding them and letting them go may not be easy. Illness has its payoff in attention, rest, social value, and other benefits. What pluses does it have for you? What price are you willing to pay for health?

D. Are you enjoying everything you are doing? You can be happy all the time if you are willing to take things as they come.

There are two ways of meeting difficulties: you alter the difficulties or you alter yourself to meet them.

Your healthy body is hanging in the closet of your thoughts. Get ready for custom fitting at a moment's notice. Look past the price tag of what has gone before. Realize you deserve a healthy body. Surround yourself with people, places and energy that promote good health.

As my mom used to say, "It's time to clean the closet when it won't close no more." So start pitching, reorganizing, and stop looking for reasons to keep the hat that says, "Don't eat yellow snow." And like real closets, remember, the job is never done, it just gets easier the more often you clean it.

Ledge Living

Old myth: Always do what is comfortable.

New myth: Take risks. Try something and fail instead of doing nothing and calling it success.

Judy Pearson

If you are willing to go the extra mile, give a little more, walk a bigger path, you are a candidate for Ledge Living.

Here are 8 steps to take if you are willing to live on the healthy ledge of life.

1. Don't lament the past. Move on. My kids tell me I have a very short memory. I don't know if they are right. I can't remember. When I concentrate on what I am doing this moment, I forget the trivial day to day facts. Learn from your lessons of the past and set your sights just a slight bit higher than you have ever done before.

2. Use the salvage system when things don't work out as you planned. Salvage what worked and discard what didn't. Don't panic or plunge into a blue funk. You are one mistake closer to being a healthy winner.

3. Ignore little disappointments and irritations in order to meet your larger goals. The adaptable person learns to live with a certain amount of inconvenience, disappointment, dismay, embarrassment, discourage-

ment and antagonism. Focus on enjoying peace of mind through daily practice of meditation. That's a large enough goal — for a lifetime.

4. Develop innovative techniques to be aware of the world around you. Think of how you can make your life exciting, fulfilling and fun.

5. Acknowledge what you can change, accept what you cannot change, and act with the wisdom to know the difference.

6. Don't identify failures in yourself. Others are more than willing to point them out for you. There is no such thing as failure, only mistakes or wrong turns. Your next turn may be just what you are looking for — and you couldn't have arrived without taking that last wrong turn.

7. Create your style for life. Read a lot. Constantly learn new things. There are only three fear-busters: Love, knowledge and action.

8. Only 2% of our fears are worth dealing with. Don't waste your time with fears. Write down the way you want a given situation to turn out and focus on it, be prepared for other outcomes, and be flexible in dealing with life.

Trying on Many Coats

"Experience is the name everyone gives to their mistakes."

Oscar Wilde

The only way to find out what you want is by trying on new experiences. We talk about commitment to spiritual excellence, to seeing our lives change for the better, but how few of us actually take the necessary action to achieve it. Webster defines excellence as "Something in which one excels." Common usage implies that excellence is the ability to be superior (the best we can). Which is not about being superior to anyone, but striving to be superior to what you thought you could be. As we strive to achieve excellence in spiritual growth, accepting the omniscient, omnipresent, omnipotent Spirit within, it takes clear personal focus and an ability to manage your own spiritual development.

Here are nine tools to help you stay focused on your goals and on successfully achieving them. Follow these steps and you will be nine steps closer to spiritual excellence.

1. Know what you want. The only thing you need to know is what you want and that you deserve to have anything your heart desires. "Ask and the door will open." Jesus' idea of opening doors is the same as trying on many coats. When we are clear about what we want to obtain, Spirit always provides.

2. Be specific. When you clarify and focus on a specific idea, it takes on significance. If you expect to get what you want in a restaurant, you tell the waiter exactly what you want. Just saying, "I want some food" could result in some interesting meals.

3. Write down your goals. Even if you know in your mind exactly what you want to have happening in your life, the act of writing it down moves it from a passive goal to an active one.

4. List the benefits and satisfactions of achieving your goals. Make a list of the good things that will happen when your goal is reached. Imagine the way it will feel as a part of your new experience.

5. List the losses or dissatisfactions of achieving your goals. What is the trade-off? A healthy mind practices being aware of both the negative and positive aspects of any action. Get your fears out in the open. It is easier to deal with them and make appropriate decisions.

6. Set a date. Mark your calendar. Don't fall prey to "I'll do it tomorrow." Would you allow your dentist to constantly put off your appointment? Well, okay, maybe not your dentist. How about your masseuse? Would you like her to keep postponing your appointment? Then why accept that kind of procrastination from yourself?

7. Act in silence. Relaxation and meditation is the most powerful tool you can use to change your thoughts and bring peace to any situation. Take time out to rejuvenate, evaluate, and give thanks for where you are on your path.

8. Visualize the results. Visualize what you want.

Imagine what it is like to have what you want from tip to toe. Feel, sense, smell, own your goals. You deserve them. Whether it's a relationship, job, peace of mind, money, or good health flowing in your life, you must experience it from within before you experience it externally.

9. Seek out the opportunity. Keep your eyes and ears open, become aware of your first response of, "No," and listen to your small voice within to determine whether you are coming from fear or common sense.

Somebody said it couldn't be done-
But he, with a grin, replied
He'd never be one to say it couldn't be done—
Leastways, not till he tried.
So he buckled right in, with a trace of a grin:
By golly, he went right to it.
He tackled The Thing That Couldn't Be Done!
And he couldn't do it.

Anonymous

To learn about other suggestions for staying focused on your goals, turn to the resource list in the back of the book.

No Pain, No Gain!
Push it! Push it!

"When I feel like exercise, I lie down until the feeling goes away."

Fred Allen, American comedian

Everyone knows the importance of exercise. It's good for you. But who wants to do it? Our awareness of our bodies as a barometer of life has been drastically tipped off keel. We believe mechanics fix cars and doctors are here to fix bodies. If we take a car to the shop with 50,000 miles on the speedometer, never had an oil change, the tires are bald and running on the rims, the fenders are all dented, and the transmission is operating on one gear, should we expect the mechanic to start from scratch to repair what could have been taken care of by daily preventive practice?

Exercise, diet, environmental awareness, and quality silent time is the combination-practice in action that helps create a healthy body. Exercise is not about making you as strong as Arnold Schwarzenegger. The goal is to arouse the body into relaxation and stimulate the glands into their natural cleansing action and balance.

I still get caught up in my thoughts with worries of family situations or the business of life, and I forget I have a body to attend to. The simple act of walking, bringing the right leg forward with the left arm and the left leg forward with the right arm relieves stress and brings balance to the brain. I now walk three to four miles a day and run after my two year old grand-daughter Wensdai when I have the privilege to be with her.

I learned some helpful steps to getting enough exercise. Keep trying different forms until one suits you.

Check with your physician before any exercise program. But don't use not checking with authorities as an excuse for doing nothing about an exercise practice.

Some suggestions for getting started:

1. **Decide to exercise.** As simple as this seems, the conscious decision must be, "I am going to exercise for one-half hour, five days a week at 7:00 in the morning." Simply making this commitment sets the stage for a successful program. Start out slow. Don't try to run a marathon the first time you go out. Keep in mind, just as it took an accumulation of thoughts to create this body, your body has to get used to the changes — down to the cellular level.

2. **Make it social.** If you commit to meeting a friend or family member for a walk or a slow jog, you are more inclined to stay on a regular schedule than if you are alone. If this would be an aid to your consistent exercise, then locate someone who can exercise with you, and the two or three of you (as the case may be) can get healthier together.

3. **Join a health club** and follow its exercise regimen. If you pay money for something, you are much more inclined to stay with it regularly. Shop for a

health club, take out a trial membership. If everyone there is interested in slick greased muscle mass and you haven't worked out in years, trust me, this will not inspire you.

The bennies? If you are overweight at all, you will begin to shed pounds. But the important results are a new sense of self esteem and an energy increase.

There will be significant changes occurring in your body's chemical analysis. Both a healthy diet and moderate exercise are powerful tools toward bringing you a lifestyle that is in balance with nature.

10 Amusing Excuses for Not Exercising

A group of physicians were asked to share a few of the "outrageous" excuses patients have given them for not getting around to exercising. Do any of these fit you?

1 . "I can't exercise because I am out of shape."
2. " Well, if I go and exercise...any time that I will live longer l will have spent exercising, and therefore I will have wasted it."
3. "My hair might get messed up."
4. "I can't exercise. An earthquake drained my pool."
5. "I have only so many heartbeats left and I don't want to waste them."
6. "I can't exercise because my leotard shrunk."
7. "I can't exercise because my kids will laugh at me."
8. "I can't exercise. I have a hyena." (He meant hernia.)
9. "I don't go to the gym because the TV is always on something I don't want to watch."
10. "Working out makes my boyfriend jealous."

What's your excuse? Mine? "I don't want to give my mother the satisfaction of saying that I'm taking care of myself."

High Hopes

*"Life without idealism is empty indeed. We just have
hope or starve to death."*

Pearl S. Buck

What tells that little ol' ant he can move that rubber
tree plant? Everyone knows an ant can't move a rubber
tree plant! Right? Or so the song goes.

I felt like the little ant who couldn't when I was
facing the prospect of changing my life-long habits.
When I decided not to take chemotherapy, I really felt
like an ant with no ant hill.

We can learn something from our friend the ant.
Amazingly, ants can carry hundreds of times their
weight everyday, while going the equivalent of hundreds of miles from home. Yet they always (somehow)
stay focused on where they are going and on finding
their way back. What magic ingredient does it take to
keep us focused? When I decided to change my thinking about cancer, I felt like it was an uphill struggle. I
didn't know where to begin. I had no idea I could do it,
but I was set on fire with the desire I had at 19 years
old and then again at 40 to LIVE life. Here are some of
the tools I learned to use:

1. Spend a day focused on your thoughts. Okay,
less than a day will work. How about starting with a
minute or two? Listen to yourself and the world you
have created around you.

2. Be authentic. Learn to know what the truth is for

you...then speak it. We all grow when we hear the truth about a situation. Even if it isn't what others want to hear. Whatever and wherever you are today is enough. It is the authenticness of you. Tomorrow you will be different.

3. Own your beliefs. They are truly the only thing you can call your own. Let go of the beliefs that no longer serve you. Use self talk to change the harmful patterns you are ruling your life with now.

4. Take time out. The power of silence is the best tool for change. Use relaxation-imagery-meditation to solve problems, become aware of your body, and bring focus and achievement to your goals.

5. Copy and complete the **Creative Mind** order form on the next page.

Look for the resources located at the back of this book for more ways to raise your expectations and high hopes.

Creative Mind, Unlimited

The Original Storehouse of Infinite Good
ORDER BLANK

Ship to:_____
(Your name)

For Immediate Delivery:

Order whatever you desire from Life. Select it. Write it down. Sorry, no C.O.D. shipments can be accepted. The mental and emotional equivalent of your desire must accompany this order.

Caution: Doubt, fear, uncertainty, discouragement, self-pity and pessimism automatically cancel this order!

This Order Subject To: Your thinking! It is not what you say you want but it is the tendency of your thought about what you want that will deliver your order. Examine your order carefully for accuracy. Use the "I want" (I welcome a new thought) order list below.

Example: I want: harmony in the home, so I welcome a new thought about (peace, or loving Fred, or paying the bills.)

So I welcome a new thought: I wipe out limited thinking by saying "No" to old mental reactions.

I wipe out limited thinking by saying: "I release all thought of argument: there is no idea in my mind which denies the love-ability of Fred, for he is also a divine being of LOVE and light".. *or*... "There are no blocks to the prompt, easy payment of obligations."

100

Creative Mind, Unlimited

The Original Storehouse of Infinite Good
ORDER BLANK

I want: _____

So I welcome a new thought about: _____

_____

I wipe out limited thinking by saying: _____

_____

❖ ❖ ❖

I want: _____

So I welcome a new thought about: _____

_____

I wipe out limited thinking by saying: _____

_____

❖ ❖ ❖

I want: _____

So I welcome a new thought about: _____

_____

I wipe out limited thinking by saying: _____

_____

Laugh At Yourself

"We are all here for a spell, so get all the laughs you can."

Will Rogers

My granddaughter, Wensdai (who is learning to read) and I were in the department store. She picked up a package from my cart. "Q-U-E-E-N S-I-Z-E." "Why, Grandma," she said, to the amusement of everyone nearby, "You're the same size as our mattress."

Someone once said that using humor is like changing a diaper — it's not a permanent fix but it makes everyone feel better. Taking life lightly can go a long way in helping you recover your health or becoming healthier. If you are ever caught in the pit of despair, the first thing to do is to laugh. Even if you have to fake it at first. Pretty soon your body will catch up with what the mind is trying to tell it and both will be on the way back to balance. When we laugh we share the spirit of ourselves with the world.

Remember your foot crossing the threshold, after you told yourself this is going to be a great day? After your good morning greeting, your co-worker replies, "Oh, it would be a great day if it weren't for the fact that shipping is all screwed up, the filing system around here sucks, and I can't get a decent cup of coffee." You have a choice. You can join the energy of chaos or bring in humor and laugh at your world. You may reply with, "Well, I can only fix the coffee! That reminds me, did you hear the one about..."

Norman Cousins' book *Anatomy Of An Illness* repeatedly states that the mental attitudes of patients have a lot to do with the course of their dis-ease and illustrates this theme with examples taken from clinical materials. Also introduced is the power of laughter and its healing effects when assisting the body in getting well.

> *"I made the joyous discovery that ten minutes of genuine belly laughter had a anesthetic effect and would give me at least two hours of pain free sleep."*

Norman Cousins

Just as negative emotions produce negative chemical changes in the body, so the positive emotions produce positive chemical changes. Dr. O. Carl Simonton has written a number of books and papers citing stress as the cause of cancer. Many other studies show that moods of depression impair the body's immunological functions.

Three Suggestion for Increasing Your Health Through Humor:

1. Look for humor in every situation. There is always a lighter side to the darkest circumstance. Take note of what you see and comment on it if it is appropriate. Store it away for future use.

2. Collect humorous stories. How? Ask for them. Next time you are in a line, or in the waiting room, try

this. Talk with the person next to you. Ask them, "Say, I'll bet you see some funny things happen in your line of work." I can guarantee the answer. "No, nothing funny ever happens around here. "Don't be put off. Wait a few precious moments, then typically you will hear a story. "There was this one time, though…" Listen carefully, and as soon as you have a chance, write it down. I used to ask, "How was school today?" My kids always replied okay, fine. What I could have asked was, "Tell me something funny that happened today." If the child says nothing funny happened, then you are ready to tell something humorous you saw or heard while standing in line at the grocery store or at the office.

Here's a story to start your collection:

I asked my local optometrist's assistant what funny things have happened at work? She gave me this smile…Most optometrist have a guaranteed replacement for glasses that are damaged by accident. A woman inquiring about the guarantee ask if her glasses could be replaced after one of her twins put them in the microwave, while she was correcting his brother. She placed the wad of plastic on the counter with a sheepish look in her eye. They were replaced.

3. The next time you are in a potentially stressful situation, acknowledge how much responsibility you choose to take for what you are hearing. "I accept responsibility for…I am willing to do what it takes to change… "

I have listed resources at the back of this book to get you started laughed yourself to wellness.

Devoted Eating

"There is no love sincerer than the love of food."

George Bernard Shaw

Let's throw away the word diet. It has lost its value and meaning to wellness. *Webster's Dictionary* defines diet as: A way of living, manner of living in regard to food and drink. Changing your way of life and your relationship with food can be a challenge.

When I started cooking whole grains, rices, barley, wheat, and millet, fresh vegetables and fruits, my teenagers headed for the hills of Burger King.

I used the macrobiotic cancer prevention diet to clean the toxins from my body. A few years later, after stating for many years that diet had nothing to do with cancer prevention or care, the American Cancer Society Cancer Prevention Diet approved a very similar way of eating.

Three Things I Learned About Diet:
1. Nature provides food to nourish our bodies. Green beans don't grow in cans. Milk is not formed in the dairy case. And Rice-a-Roni is not a staple.

2. We have an undeniable spiritual connection to food. The combination of the nutrients of food and the feeling food gives us nourishes our bodies on a much deeper level than we are aware.

Our bodies sense food before we consciously eat it. The spirit within us connects with sights, sounds, smells, tastes and — most of all — feeling of the food.

3. We are born of earth and water. We are connected to our source, our supply, by the food we eat, the air we breathe, and the energy we use to prepare a meal. Grabbing a bite to eat on the run...instant, just add water, prepared foods...skipping a meal (which is something I was never good at)...weakens our feeling of connection with our source.

I have designed a special Devoted Eating Meditation allowing one to experience a deeper consciousness about food. Try it. Let me know what you think.

The resource list in the back of this book is a guide to places and people who can support you in your quest for changing your way of living with food and drink.

Devoted Eating Meditation

We eat the same way as we lead our lives. Are we unconscious? Are we consuming the Universe or are we receiving Universal nourishment?

Become mindful of what you eat and of the many processes going on in the mind and body by:

Step One – See your food. The colors, textures, and feel.

Step Two – Intend to reach for it. Become aware of your intention. It is the intention that drives the body into action to reach for a bite of food.

Step Three – Become aware of the sensation of touching. Notice how you feel...

Step Four – Become aware of lifting, the weight, size and shape — how does it feel in your hand?

Step Five – Become aware of opening your mouth.

Step Six – Become aware of putting the food into your mouth.

Step Seven – Become aware of lowering your arm.

Step Eight – Feel the texture of the food.

Step Nine – Become aware of chewing.

Step Ten – Give special attention to the tasting.

Step Eleven – Become aware of the swallowing.

Step Twelve – Give thanks for the process of life.

Be Aware...Be Alert...Be Alive

The Wizardry of Awe Counting

"Be an Awe Counter. The more you praise, the more you raise. It has been proven that thankfulness brings wellness."

Judy Pearson

Loving yourself body and soul, just the way it is right now, is awe counting and can seem like a challenge. Overweight, underweight, too smooth, too wrinkled, too short, too tall, too young, too old, too big, too little, too cute, too ugly reflects the American obsession and distortion of how fitness and wellness are defined. How can we appreciate the instrument-body when we are bombarded by how it is never enough? When we treat this bag of bones, brains, and blood, as a powerful expression of Love or God, we treat it with respect and that creates a state of grace with nature.

I was a superwoman swishing through life. Yes, Super Stella here. Chauffeur, cook, organizer, non-working mother (what a joke!) and artist. I thought everything I did had to be done yesterday. I took no time for me to stop and say Awe. I believed the message that most women get early in life that no matter how much you do, how efficient you are, you must never let anyone know you are enough unto yourself.

It's a message all people get, yet most women are willing to hide out in being second best in order to soothe the male ego and keep peace in the family.

Ralph Waldo Emerson wrote, "What we commonly call man, the eating, drinking, planting, counting man does not, as we know him, represent himself, but misrepresents himself. Him we do not respect, but the soul, whose organ he is, would he let it appear through his action, would make our knees bend." When we know the nature of ourselves, attuned to nature, our unique expression of Spirit is powerful.

Take a moment to reflect on the enormous complexity and simplicity of millions of body cells that die, eliminate, grow, change, and reproduce every day. We don't concentrate or give conscious thought to tell our hair to grow, and yet all the ingredients of blood, oil, nerves, carotene, and air produce thousands of hairs continuously. It's an Awe even if you only have one hair on your head. The Awe and wonder of this act of nature is a miracle. Awe is thanksgiving. Smelling the roses. Counting awes in your life.

It's quiet, a gentle breeze touches the hair on your arm. The sun's warmth and glow penetrate every cell of your body. As you watch the ribbons of glowing color slowly change, then settle into the western horizon, a feeling of relaxation, completeness, oneness, Awe, comes over your body. It's the Awes and humor that stir a sense of wellness in us.

Awe counting is not only about looking for things to be thankful for. It is also about how we nurture ourselves. We see, hear, smell, and feel the anguish of the world from the media of radio, television, newspaper, and Gracie Gossips that bombard us constantly. Our subjective-subconscious mind is like a giant sponge, constantly running over a collection of thoughts or ideas. It makes no judgments, it draws no conclusions, it simply soaks in everything it sees and hears for further use. While this sub-mind sponge is collecting data, the conscious mind tries to think, rationalize, and organize with a mind that is connected to a large barometer, the body, and every thought that has feeling reacts on the body.

We become more God-like, more in-tuned with the omnipresent energy that is in all things as we become aware of the wonders of life and love.

Five Steps to Awesomeness:

1. Look at the world around you as a picture painted especially for you by God. Let the picture you see be what you show everyone around you.
2. Open your heart to compassion for others and the process of life they may be experiencing now. Remember that you are here to share light...the light of your spirit within you.
3. Gaze at God once every hour. Find something to be thankful for in all situations. The old phrase "Praise the Lord" takes on a new meaning when you can realize the wonder of the omnipresent God and its teachings.
4. Do manual labor that you might not ordinarily do. Do it not for the exercise but for the sheer knowing that this is as important to sharing spirit as the purpose of your goals.
5. Find books, tapes, and videos that stimulate the feeling of thanks and thanksgiving. Listed at the back of this book are suggestion for increasing your awareness of Awe Counting.

"When it breathes through his intellect, it is genius; when it breathes through his will, it is virtue: when it breathes through his affection, it is love."

Author Unknown

Leaning Out

*"Believing in yourself and liking yourself
is all part of good looks."*

Shirley Lord

Cancer will affect at least one in four. That is worse than Russian roulette. The National Cancer Institute for years denied that nutrition had anything to do with this disease. They have since taken a 180-degree about-face. Get in touch with the American Cancer Society for a recommended cancer-prevention diet.

If you are serious about reducing your risk of getting cancer, my suggestion is that you do the following: Choose your own style of food intake, just make sure it is from food that is alive and fresh.

The following dietary guidelines are prepared by the American Institute for Cancer Research and endorsed by the National Academy of Sciences:

1. Reduce the intake of dietary fat both saturated and unsaturated to a maximum level of 20-30 percent of the total calories. This can be done by limiting the use of meat, trimming away its excess fat, avoiding fried foods, and cutting down on butter, cream, salad dressings, and so forth.

2. Increase the consumption of nutrients:

Fresh fruits of every kind — find your favorites and try new varieties too.

Fresh vegetables — green, yellow, red or purple — vary your intake but head mostly for the green and yellow for cancer prevention.

Whole grains, grain cereals— grains such as brown rice, millet, oats, barley, and wheat are an excellent source of nutrients as well as bulk.

3. Research vitamins and minerals. Be knowledgable about how they work to heal the body. Get in touch with a naturopath or herbalist. Learn what your body needs to stay well or overcome illness.

Stop these practices:

1. Stop all use of tobacco. It restricts the blood from flowing through your body easily. It slows down your reactions and thinking process.

2. Substantially reduce your fat intake to 20-30% of your calories or less. Intakes of dietary fat are convincingly associated with cancers in the hormone axis — that being breast, uterus, prostate, ovaries, and as well as cancer of the colon.

3. Eat two carrots and two apples (or more) per day as additional sources of dietary fiber and beta-carotene.

4. Eat some broccoli, cauliflower, or leafy greens three (or more) times per week, as this family of vegetables has specific ingredients that protect against colon cancer and other types of cancer.

5. Take multiple vitamin and mineral supplements to assist the body with the change in diet.

6. Avoid smoked, pickled, and salt cured food. These all contain nitrosamine as well as other agents proven to cause cancer in animals.

Increase your intake of the following five nutrients

known to protect against cancer: betacarotene, vitamin A, vitamin C, vitamin E, selenium, and dietary fiber. Follow your medical practitioner's advice when taking these substances.

The New Pasta Diet

Just walk pasta bakery without stopping.
Walk pasta candy store without stopping.
Walk pasta ice cream shop without stopping.

Pricing Success

"When we realize we don't know who we are or what we know, we are open to knowing."

Judy Pearson

One of the exciting wonders of recognizing our seeming need for control and beginning to let it go is the weightlessness of the anticipation that everything and anything is possible. Being aware that nothing is gained materially, physically, or mentally without paying a price is one of the first lessons I learned when I began to change what I wanted to experience in my world. I wanted to have a happier marriage, a relationship open to communication. The price? Speaking up, telling the truth about who I think I am right now. I wanted to be a spiritual consultant. The price? Focused studying and a willingness to let go of what I thought was the meaning of being spiritual.

Sometimes it's the incentive, the goal, that means the most to us.

A hairdressing client of mine told me of her husband's recovery after surgery. She had recounted the doctor's orders to her husband, saying, "In six months you'll be able to walk up two flights of stairs, lift 20 pounds, and you can resume normal sexual activity." Her husband responded, "If I'd known about the sex, I would have had the surgery a long time ago!"

"The fire department quickly brought the fire under control, but not before the building had burned to the ground."

The Oregonian

What is the price you would be willing to pay for a better career, more loving relationship, or healthier body? What do you want to happen? What are the rewards when they do happen? What do you need to let go of? Are you willing to pay the price?

Go With The Flow

Okay, I thought, as I listened to the announcement: Your flight to Dallas/Fort Worth has been delayed an hour. More time to wonder why I am going to the National Speakers Association conference. I spent all this money, turned down jobs for this time period, and now I am wondering why I'm going. Should I go? Maybe I could wait another year. An affirmation I share with clients and friends when they are in doubt kept coming to mind. "When what you thought was impossible comes together without much effort, *go with the flow.*"

The flight from the Orient passed customs and boarded. Two Korean businessmen smiled as they took their seats. "Well, I'll be catching a few winks. They don't understand English nor I Korean. Great. Cross your arms and doze time."

Dressed to the nines and looking refreshed after an eight-hour flight from Korea to Portland, heading for Dallas/Fort Worth via Atlanta, a national cemetery architect, Mr. Duk Suk, asked me for the time. Holding his wristwatch next to mine both were showing identical times, and I knew this person either wanted to speak to me or sell me a watch.

Constantly flipping through a translation book my Korean friend found questions, wrote them down and waited for my reply. "How long was the flight to Dallas? What do you do for a living? Do you have a son? When is your birthday?" I don't tell my friends, let alone strangers, how old I am, yet I wrote down the numbers and explained their placing. He began to add them up (not a good sign) then scrolled something in Korean along side. Reading my numbers..." Mmmm berrey-gooood career type, mmmm berrey-gooood body type, mmm berrey-gooood family type." He then took my palm and began to read the various lines. "Long lifeline...mmmm berrey-good talent, long line...career line connects to your heart line...mmmm berrey good..." He then pushed back my hair and read my forehead and profile. Telling me again, "Mmmm berrey-goood," he wrote on the napkin "You are power and supportive type." He was right. Thank you God. I felt that truth deep inside me, I knew that all my doubts were just that — doubts — and that my passion and purpose in assisting people in learning preventive health care practices was the reason I was on this flight.

It occurred to me I might have gotten more sleep on this flight and missed a wonderful gift. Mr. Duk Suk and I may have never shared our spirit and I wouldn't have heard what I needed to hear at that very moment. I needed that boost and Spirit provided the time and place. All I had to do was listen. Are you listening?

Three keys to listening for life's lessons.
1. Take time to listen to yourself.
2. Be open to opportunities to share.
3. Go with the flow (even on an airplane.)

My longtime friend and fellow counselor Jean Celia says:

If It Doesn't Flow, Let It Go!

Part V

Meditations for the Stressful Times

R.I.M.: The Art of Relaxation-Imagery-Meditation

"Relax your thoughts and allow the free flow of the Life Essence, in and through you, and your body will respond to its healing activity."

Ernest Holmes

I believe the key to renewing and maintaining a healthy life is taking time to take care of your body and mind. When I heard about meditation, visions of a guru with legs crossed, sitting on a pillow, breathing incense, and humming "oooooommmmmm" flashed before my eyes. Yet meditation is much more. It is the most powerful way I've found to assisting the body to wellness.

When we are ill, whether it is a cold, flu, or cancer, the mind and the body are in a state of confusion. Thoughts are going a hundred miles an hour, controlled by fear. Or they're dragging along soaked in the pain of the moment. A relaxation-imagery tape helped me calm down and get a grip on my panic. I practiced being still for the first time in my life. It was uncomfortable at first to learn the skill of doing nothing. Later I found that teaching others to meditate was made easier if the student learned to relax and visualize, until they slipped into a state of meditation comfortably. The world of meditation methods is unlimited. Music, birds singing, the ocean, boat sails catching the wind, all of nature's sounds help to calm us and bring us back to our true nature of being human and connected to the earth.

Classes on relaxation, imagery, and meditation became my specialty. I now teach people that meditation is more effective when you realize there is no perfect right way to do it. Meditation is about finding time in quiet, in contemplation, and letting the mind and body renew and rejuvenate. Different forms may include walking the dog, going fishing, taking a motorcycle ride, sitting by a stream in silence, or listening to the sound of silence. Music or visualization, imagery, calms you to a point of acceptance and can be a great help to the first time student. One student said to me, "You took the wee-waa out of meditation and brought it into my daily life."

The rewards of the daily practice of R.I.M. are surprising and well worth the time and effort. By going deeper in contemplation I can allow the Spirit within me to guide me in my daily life.

Do you know the positive benefits of regular R.I.M. practice?

The benefits of meditation practice have been long extolled by health practitioners, but only recently have volunteer meditators been carefully studied under controlled circumstances. The evidence is now coming in and we have an accumulation of experience. I will share a few of the conclusions drawn by researchers who have monitored the meditators' responses and published their research findings.

1. Deep conscious relaxation: By observing changes in brain wave patterns and other physiological conditions, we know it is possible through meditation to experience conscious relaxation which is more complete than that experienced during the ordinary sleep state. People actually can experience complete rest while remaining "awake" — that is, while being totally conscious.

2. Stress reduction: When we use deep relaxation, slowing of breathing patterns and activity of internal organs, emotions become settled and mental activity becomes refined. Meditators reveal a reduction of blood lactate levels indicating a lessening of stress in the body, deduced from an examination of blood samples. The harmful effects of hypertension have been widely reported, not the least of which can be elevated blood pressure, migraine headaches, and interference with normal functioning of glands and organs. Many meditators with a history of high blood pressure have been able to reduce blood pressure to a safe level by meditating on a regular daily schedule for the relaxation benefits.

3. Concentration improves: Easy flow of attention to the purpose at hand is concentration. During meditation our attention is naturally drawn inward, without interferences from unwanted thoughts or emotional surge. After meditation we find it easier to concentrate on projects and relationships. In this way we can be

more productive and functional. The conscious exercise of concentration during waking hours enables us to meditate more effectively.

4. Increased orderly thinking: When super-conscious forces prevail during meditation thought streams are aligned automatically. Chaos and conflict can dissipate in the body and mind. After meditation, because of the relaxed awareness one experiences, thought processes tend to harmoniously arrange and the interaction between left and right hemispheres of the brain is balanced.

5. Strengthening the immune system: Confusion, despair, anxiety, fear, and loneliness contribute to weakening of the immune system, the body's defense against disease, and deterioration. Conscious relaxation and super-conscious meditation experience, on the other hand, are conducive to strengthening the immune system. Meditation, the cultivation of optimism, hope, faith, and feelings of love, has a healthy nourishing influence on the immune system.

6. Delaying the aging process: An analysis of meditators indicates that persons who meditate on a regular schedule do not show signs of aging as fast as non-meditators. Mental and emotional states are healthier, evidence of stress is minimal and the immune system is stronger.

7. Improving the quality of life: To merely exist in space and time or to cope with a seeming never-ending series of challenges is not the real purpose of living. The general improvement in mental, emotional and physical health promotes self-value. Meditators tend to enjoy life more and to have purpose and direction

in their lives.

8. Expand intelligence: Our ability to discern, to draw correct conclusions, and to perceive without error is an indication of intelligence. When thoughts and feelings are confused, when self-defeating attitudes are maintained, our ability to exercise native intelligence diminishes. Super-conscious influences experienced during and after meditation increase awareness and harmonize thoughts and emotions. Self-defeating attitudes tend to be dissolved. The result is that most meditators experience an increase in intellectual abilities.

9. Awaken intuition: Intuition is our innate ability to know by knowing. It is the ability to perceive directly on an innate level what is being looked at. When we experience a flash of insight, a gut feeling, there is an inner knowing...this is intuition. Through the use of intelligence and intuition it is possible to discern the inner side of nature and subjectively experience reality at a finer and deeper level than is sensed by perception alone.

10. Boost self-sufficiency and freedom of choice: As a result of being able to rest in the silence during meditation, an experience of self completeness is discovered. You may notice that you are no longer as dependent upon the external world as you once were.

The meditator experiences himself as a self-reliable person and is therefore able to make better wiser choices about how he chooses to live life and what he will do with his time, energies and talents. Many people have been able to make very important choices in healing and living productive lives.

11. Increased creativity: A healthy human being is by nature a problem solver and goal achiever. Removing inner restricting patterns and conditions, you can discover a pronounced increase in creative abilities. You are able to flow with the rhythms of life more easily and accomplish useful purposes with relative ease. Creativity comes easily flowing forth with ideas as we learn to relax. Buckle your divine seat belt, the possibilities are endless.

12. Increase in spiritual awareness: As a result of sound practices of meditation you can experience the real nature of yourself and your relationship to the world around you. Meditation deepens your appreciation of religious teachings, philosophy and your spiritual connection. A more pronounced sense of unity-consciousness and harmony with the Universe naturally unfolds.

13. Freedom from addictions of all kinds: The addictive personality has emotional needs which it attempts to satisfy by using and abusing substances, behaviors, or relationships which are often harmful and destructive. Even if such substances, behaviors, or relationships are not a health challenge, they still result in a diminishment of creativity and they prevent a person from exploring a wide range of possibilities in life. The symptoms of addiction vary and include overeating, undereating, alcohol and/or drug abuse, and self-defeating behavior of many kinds. The real problem is never "out there" and it is well for the person with an addictive personality disorder to realize that he is not a victim. Every person has freedom of choice. After the daily practice of meditating deeply you may

find you are able to choose wise behavior and let go of behavior that no longer suits you.

14. Humility and a sense of Awe and thanksgiving:

Meditation gives you the time needed to contemplate the wonders of the world. Each day there is a newness of awesome wonder at the things you took for granted just yesterday. There is a closer connection with the way the Universe runs and your part and purpose in it. Giving thanks each day for something in your life becomes easy and a joy.

It's fine to say, meditate for these benefits, but what do you do when you feel the world outside of you is crumbling?

On the following pages are **Meditations and Affirmations for the Stressful Times** in our lives.

Read through the meditation once then again more slowly. Put the book down, take a deep breath and just take time to let go, letting the words and the feelings sink in.

Remember, this is a practice, so don't expect to get the full benefit the first time. You are learning a new skill. The more you practice, the more skilled you will become, and the more benefits you will derive. Enjoy!

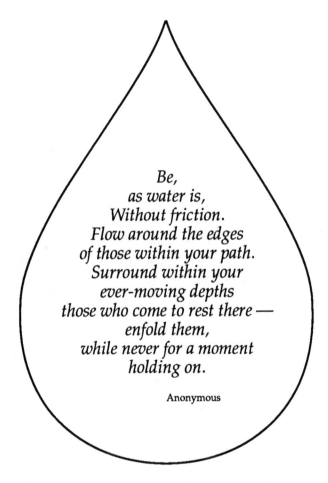

Be,
as water is,
Without friction.
Flow around the edges
of those within your path.
Surround within your
ever-moving depths
those who come to rest there —
enfold them,
while never for a moment
holding on.

Anonymous

Meditations for Stressful Times

Before you were born you had everything. You lived in a warm comfortable compartment. You were cared for, nourished; you had no worries, no fears; you were comfortable. Room service was terrific. This was a great place to live. Then one day...suddenly, you were served an eviction notice. You were pushed down a long narrow corridor that was way too small. Your head popped out, then your body came out into a colder place. Your body stretched like it had never stretched before. Your world all of a sudden had changed. Everything feels bigger, brighter, colder, louder, more chaotic.

This is your first change of life. Your first experience is the feeling of separation. Immediately your well-being depends on others. You are now on the planet earth. For the rest of your life there will be two basic emotions in your daily life: fear and love. Fear happens when you feel separated from love. Love happens when you know you are safe, whole and at one with Universal Spirit. There is no doubt that as human beings we will experience feelings of separation in stressful times. The following meditations and affirmations are designed to help you focus on the positive aspects and the unity of all life.

Meditation for the Stressful Times of Employment

Take a deep breath...hold it to the count of 8...now count backwards...slowly letting go of your breath, count...8...7...6....5...4...3...2...1...

Let your shoulders relax...let any tension melt as you become one with what supports you...Let go... and go deeper...and deeper...with each breath go deeper...

Envision yourself near a crystal clear pond in the middle of nature...all around you is sunshine and beautiful colors of natural things. As you come closer to the pond you notice how clear and clean it is...you look deeply into the depths of the water and find a small precious stone...You notice an inscription on the stone written especially for you...you read it carefully... knowing that whatever its meaning, it is made clear to you...Right now, take a deep breath...relax... notice the reflection on the top of the water...It is the most important message of your lifetime...it is you reflecting as spirit...sharing your spirit-self with positive, healthy, life giving words and deeds...

What does it look like for you to live as a full expression of life...What is your life purpose?...Take time now to explore the unlimited possibilities...Ask Spirit to guide you in finding and expressing your life's purpose. Every labor leads to a fuller expression of the self...Let Spirit speak to you...You are free to be healthy, whole and full of life...You deserve to be happy in your life's work...accept a happy life now... give thanks for the resources that have brought you to this place and time in your life...you have selected Life...relax and live it...relax...take a moment to be still...

Affirmation

I listen and follow my heart. I choose to express as a spirit in every area of my life. I am free to choose life.

A Meditation for the Stressful Times of Divorce

Take a cleansing breath...This is the first day of the rest of your life. Your breath relaxes you and you let go of all thoughts. Focus on the ease and comfort of letting go...let your muscles smooth and become supple. Imagine yourself in nature...the warm soft glow of the sun on your skin...the air fresh...the colors of green, blue, yellow, brown surround you...

There is a path to follow...as you walk along admiring nature, you see before you a thin cloth veil. The veil ripples in the wind...it represents denial....it represents the feelings that seem to separate us... sometimes we believe our feelings and thoughts are not going to be validated or accepted, that we are not to be loved.

Lift the veil and see the true story of love in all areas, surrounding your life. Relax...take a breath... Allow yourself to face the truth...to face the facts about what is going on in your life. You make decisions easily, effortlessly. There is nothing to fear...let go and let the spirit within guide you...protect you...express through you...Now let go and forgive...let go...feel your strength...let go...feel your power...You are fully living your life...as you unite with spirit know that you are supported...You are safe...relax...stay in the silence...be still...

Affirmation

I let go of fear and know that I am supported with all that I need and want in life. I face life easily. I accept the world just the way it is and just the way it is becoming.

A Meditation for the Stressful Times at the Holidays

In the silence of this moment take in life-giving breath. Breathe out...let go...slow down your body... feel your body let go...in this moment allow your mind, body, and spirit to come together...Say to yourself...The eternal intelligence within guides me in letting go of judgment, worry, fear, anger, or guilt. I let go of all old stories...I wipe the slate clean...from this moment on I choose life and I celebrate holidays with peace and love. You now choose only life to unfold perfectly...Accept love, understanding, and patience for yourself....now accept all people in your life with love, understanding and patience...let go...and know that you celebrate life everyday just the way it is unfolding...take a breath...breathe life and peace into your world...in the silence of the moment be still and freely send your spirit to people you have met and will meet...for Spirit is pure love. Be still...let go...

Affirmation

I choose to celebrate life today and everyday. I accept love, peace, understanding and patience as life unfolds in this moment.

A Meditation for the Stressful Times of Personal Illness or Injury

Allow yourself time now to snuggle in a chair...get comfortable...take a deep cleansing breath...this is time for you to take care of you...Close your eyes...let your jaw drop...let your shoulders down....feel your arms as they let go and become light...Imagine for a moment that your whole body is supported by clouds of soft rejuvenating mist...Knowing that every thing you hear, touch, taste, breathe, affects your level of wellness, this is your time to focus on healing and wholeness...let go of guilt and worry...spirit only knows you as perfect...now is the time for you to know your perfection...you are enough just the way you are right now...

Your experience of illness is just nature's way of saying slow down...take time to enjoy life...it's the only one you have at the moment. Imagine for a moment a healing energy taking form as a ball of light...this light is filled with pure love.

Wherever you direct this light, it heals...allowing your body's own intelligence to heal and make you healthy, clear to the cellular level...Take time now to direct this nurturing ball of light to any place in your body that is in need of ease...feel that focused energy begin to relax the area and bring peace to your entire body...

Relax and go deeper...and deeper...be still...you are love...

Affirmation

I am in charge of my healthy mind and my healthy body. I now choose a happy, healthy life.

Meditation for the Stressful Times of Forgiveness

Take a deep breath...this is your time to let go...
Tense your muscles...let go...relax them...tightening
individual muscles of the body for the count of 10.
Now relax, releasing the muscles promptly to a relaxed
state. Isolate each muscle in your body, visualize and
focus...directing soothing energy to every part of your
body...if there is any discomfort, send that area healing, soothing energy to help it relax...let go...Imagine
directing a healing beam of light to the memories in the
body of past hurts...to the tension you carry from past
hurts....send a message to every muscle that it is safe
now to relax...Remembering that unpleasant memories
are only thoughts...you are in control of your life and
your thoughts...tell your body you are now here for
it...with the body-mind and spirit energy united,
choose to heal old memory wounds now...give your
body and mind permission to forgive whomever may
come to mind...you may not choose to forget...with
forgiveness you can drop the heavy baggage that has
kept you down for so long...you gain new strength,
understanding and a deepening sense of love for
yourself and others...take time now to...go
deeper...focus on love...and let go now...be still...

Affirmation

I am free. I open my heart to the world of love. I practice the art of forgiveness moment by moment.

Decide to Forgive

For resentment is negative
Resentment is poisonous
Resentment diminishes
and devours the self
Be the first to forgive,
To smile and take the first step,
And you will see happiness bloom
On the face of your human brother and sister.
Be always the first
Do not wait for others to forgive
For by forgiving
You become the master of fate
The fashion of life
The doer of miracles
To forgive is the highest, most beautiful form of love.
In return you will receive untold peace and happiness.

Here is the program for achieving a truly forgiving heart:
Sunday: Forgive yourself.
Monday: Forgive your family.
Tuesday: Forgive your friends and associates.
Wednesday: Forgive across economic lines within your own nation.
Thursday: Forgive across cultural lines of your own nation.
Friday: Forgive across political lines within your own nation.
Saturday: Forgive across other nations.

Meditation for the Stressful Times of Change in the Family

Closing your eyes...take a breath...breathe in the goodness of life. Letting go...the body relaxes into itself. Muscle by muscle, the body begins to smooth, and become supple. When fear, yabuts and mind chatter come to mind simply remember it is only a thought and let it go.

Universal Spirit IS LOVE, it is in and through all things. Accepting change...accepting the newness of life as it is evolving and becoming is made easier when we unite and let Spirit guide...let your focus be to open to change...Say to yourself...I am united with the one spirit-intelligence that knows what is best for me now...

I choose to love unconditionally all people who enter my life, just the way they are right now...I let go of expectations and accept change as part of life. Imagine your body filled with the warm feeling of LOVE. Send love to your body from the top of your head to the tip of your toes. Perfect health and peace of mind reaches every cell. Life flows easily through all that you do. In the silence, let go...contemplate peace...

Affirmation

There is no limit to what Spirit and I can do. Gratefully I accept all life's possibilities. I am unlimited. I am open to all possibilities. My life is filled with love, always moving and changing...I go with the flow.

Meditation for the Stressful Times of Transition of a Loved One

Closing your eyes...take a few deep breaths...drop your shoulders and feel the peace and silence of the moment...Slowly draw your attention to the center of your body...relax...let go...

Focusing on your breathing...let yourself go...deeper and deeper...noticing the miracle of breath. Imagine that the spark that creates the next breath is spirit...It is always there automatically, securely and endlessly...it responds. Let go of the cares and concerns of the day...let them melt away...it's time to be quiet...

Say to yourself...I am balanced and safe...I am secure...I am guided by Spirit...This moment I feel the loss of a loved one...my mind, body and spirit feel the painful void left from their passing. My physical presence is changing for I will no longer hear, smell, taste, or feel their presence outside of me...

My mind and spirit will assist me in the healing process of change...I rejoice and give thanks for the privilege of knowing a wonderful human being. I recall the lessons I have learned from being part of their life...I now take time to take care of myself knowing that life is for the living and I am here to express love and be loved.

Knowing that each life on earth is minuscule in the scheme of spirit...stay in the moment and let spirit guide you through this time to better times...Stay in the silence and give thanks...

Affirmation

I give thanks for this moment. Knowing that life moves as spirit in and through all things I adjust to the changes in life the best I know how.

Meditation for the Stressful Times with Finances

With paper money in your hand, close your eyes... take a deep breath and let it out...Feel your bodily functions become calm...let go of your concerns and worries...In the silence, in the peace, you realize that the same Spirit within you is in all people...is in all things...Universal energy is all there is...in is infinite intelligence and infinite power...and infinite love...you are one with the spirit...you cannot be separated from it...you are spirit...spirit is you...You are in connection with the one source of all life substance...

In this moment of silence, hold tightly your paper money...it is yours...reflect for a moment...what is the meaning of money in your life?...What do you use it for? Does it use you?...Clench the money...wad it up and make sure it is in the palm of the hand not able to get out...Hold it tightly...How do you feel now?...Write it down...Take time to realize that money is only one form of prosperity. God is the source of money, energy and all things. In this moment direct your healing ball of light to your heart...open your hand...open your life to the endless possibilities of wealth...

Say to yourself...Knowing that there is always enough for everyone and that I deserve the best in my life as does everyone around me, I send light and love and money to the people, places, and things in my life that support me in love...In the silence...I now reflect on all my endowments of prosperity, knowing it expands as I expand my support to good...

Affirmation

I express love in all forms to my family and friends, knowing that as I take care of myself, I can then give the best care to others.

Meditation for the Stressful Time of Vacations

Get comfortable, relax and let go...Let your shoulders drop...let your facial muscles soften...Your body becomes soft and at ease. You are in touch with your breath, your life force...Feel your breath as it brings in the new...renewing the flow of energy...renewing life...with each breath go deeper...you are safe...let go...going deeper and deeper.

No matter what appears on the outside there is a strong, stable core of perfection within. This energy by its nature is a power-filled healing energy. It is always moving...always toward the good. Any circumstance your thoughts have attracted to you that no longer serves, you can now release. It is only a thought...you can change your thoughts and change your experience.

Imagine for a moment you are in a place in nature ...it is a warm sunny day...feel the gentle breeze across your skin...you are relaxed...it is a place of peace...as you look around you can see the colors of nature...the waves of the grass move gently...you notice you are on a path...as you walk down the path you come to the top of a hill...you can see the valley below...it is a beautiful sight...you pause for a moment to gaze at the beauty of nature...All is in order now... perfect just the way it is right now...you are a reflection of natural beauty...perfect just the way you are...breathe in...breathe out...let go...be still and know...

Affirmation

I am guided by the Spirit within me. I am grateful knowing that I deserve the best. I act confidently, taking my rightful place, aware of how I feel as I share my world.

Meditation for the Stressful Times of Health Challenges of a Family Member

Treat yourself to a few minutes of peace...become calm...take a deep breath...let it out...let go of your body and let it sink into your chair...Imagine for a moment pouring down over your body a healing mist of white light relaxing your every organ...every cell...Let go and let the energy flow freely in and through you now...In the center of your being is an energy...a spirit...that knows everything...it is the pure intelligence...spirit...it knows how to heal...how to stay healthy...and how to overcome any apparent illness...

Universal energy is all there is...it is infinite intelligence...infinite power...infinite LOVE...you are one with Spirit now...you are one with the One Mind...the mind of the one source of all.

Let your spirit go out to anyone who is in need of a healing. No matter what the experience...remember there is nothing stronger than Spirit. There is no disease that can not be healed. There are only people who make choices. Your act of love affects the outcome of life. In this moment of silence...declare what you want and let the words and feeling go knowing right action is taking place right now...speak from your heart....let go...relax...take a deep breath...be still...

Affirmation

*My unique power, presence and perfection is
constantly expanding. As I express my spirit
I open to the calm power within.*

Meditation for the Stressful Times of Success

Find your comfortable chair, a place of quiet... take a deep breath...allow your body to fall into a deep relaxation...let go of all thoughts of worry or anxiety and focus now on the only thing that matters...There is one life, one spirit, that is life in this moment. This is most precious...outstretch your arms, lay open your body, allow every part of you to accept a new experience of life...

Say to yourself...gratefully letting go, I accept my good knowing it is done easily and effortlessly...I am success...I express love...I am one with the power that created me...I am guided...I go from success to success, from glory to glory...

You are a reflection of nature's love...feel the calmness of nature...take a deep breath...you can come here anytime in this space of silence and renew...get in touch with your breath...knowing the law of spirit always says yes...let go, trust, feel your calm soothed body come back to the room...Feel your breath... breathe ...this is your quiet time...be still and know...

Affirmation

I now allow the success formula to flow through me.
I have within me all the ingredients for success.
I am guided.

"Spirit is the spine and the skull of our developmental skeleton, and the spark of the intelligence behind it. Upon Spirit all the various scientific ribs hang beautifully and make coordinated sense; without Spirit we have fragmented nonsense."

Joseph Chilton Pearce

Thank you for allowing me to share my spirit. All any of us have is our spirit. I send my spirit to you so you may grow and teach and learn. Good health and happiness to all.

Judy

Resources and Bibliography

Allen, James, *As You Thinketh*, Largo, FL, Top Of The Mountain Publishing, 1988.

Allenbaugh, Allen, Ph.D., *Wake Up Calls*, Austin, TX, Discovery Publications, 1992.

Bradshaw, John, *Homecoming, Healing the Shame That Binds You*, New York, Bantam Books, 1993.

Chopra, Deepak, M.D., *Quantum Healing*, New York, NY, Bantam Books, 1990.

Chopra, Deepak, M.D., *Unconditional Life*, New York, NY, Bantam Books, 1991.

Elder, Jo, and M.I. Wiser, *A User's Guide to a Better Bod*, Lake Oswego, OR, One More Press, 1992.

Emerson, Ralph Waldo, *Essays by Ralph Waldo Emerson*, New York, NY, Harper & Row, 1951.

Espy, Willard R., *The Life and Works of Mr. Anonymous*, New York, NY, Hawthorne Books Inc., 1975

Fulghum, Robert, *All I Really Need to Know I Learned In Kindergarten*, New York, NY, Ivy Books, 1988.

Goldsmith, Joel S., *The Art of Meditation*, New York, NY, Harper & Row, 1990.

Harris, Thomas A., M.D., *I'm OK-You're OK*, New York, NY, Harper & Row, 1969.

Hay, Louise L., *You Can Heal Your Life, and Heal Your Body*, Santa Monica, CA, Hay House, 1984.

Holmes, Ernest, *The Science of Mind, Creative Mind and Success*, New York, NY, Dodd, Mead & Co., 1990

James, Jennifer, Ph.D., *Success is the Quality of the Journey*, New York, NY, Newmarket Press, 1986.

John-Roger, McWilliams, Peter, *Life 101*, Prelude Press, 1990.

Keyes, Jr., Ken, *The Hundredth Monkey*, Coos Bay, OR, Vision Books, 1982.

Ming-Doa, Deng, *365 Tao Daily Meditations*, New York, NY, Harper San Francisco, 1992.

Moyers, Bill, *Healing and The Mind*, New York, NY, Doubleday, 1993.

Sattilaro, Anthony J., M.D. *Recalled By Life*, Boston, MA, Houghton Mifflin Company, 1981.

Simonton, O. Carl, M.D., *Getting Well Again*, New York, NY, Bantam Books, 1981.

Peck, Scott M., M.D., *The Road Less Traveled*, New York, NY, Simon and Schuster, 1978.

Powell, S.J., *Why Am I Afraid to Tell You Who I Am?* Allen, TX, Tabor Publishing, 1969.

Radford, Rudy L., *Many Paths to God*, Wheaton, IL, The Theosophical Publishing House, 1970.

Siebert, Al, Ph.D., *The Survivor Personality*, Portland, OR, Practical Psychology Press, 1993.

Siegel, Bernie S., M.D., *Love, Medicine and Miracles*, New York, NY, Harper & Row, 1986.

Thoele, Sue Patton, *The Courage to Be Yourself*, Nevada City, CA, Pyramid Press, 1989.

Wilde, Larry, *The Larry Wilde Library of Laughter*, New York, NY, Ivy Books, 1988

Williamson, Marianne, *A Return to Love*, New York, NY, Harper Collins, 1993.

Winters, Jonathan, *Winter's Tales*, New York, NY, Random House, 1987.

Smith, Lendon, *Feed Your Body Right*, New York, NY, M. Evans, 1994.

Index

A

accept 70, 72
accepted 26
accepting 65, 84
achieving 92
acknowledge 63, 72
acknowledged 26, 64
acknowledging 22
act 73, 80
active 76
adaptable 76
affirmations 127
aging 124
AIDS 38
alternative 15
alternatives 13
American Cancer Society 15
anger 43, 45, 80
appreciating 80
arthritic 56
arthritis 38, 60
attitude 31, 49
attitudes 103
authentic 98
authenticness 99
automatically 86, 100
Awe Counter 108

B

bad stress 78
balance 94

barometer 110
beliefs 25, 99
body 106

C

cancer 13, 16, 38, 49
cancer patient 22
cancerous tumors 18
cassette tape 25
challenge 12, 84, 105
change 91, 109
changing 105
characters 26, 33
chemotherapy 13, 15, 23
children 42, 60
chiropractors 23
choice 12, 125
chronic illness 49
cleaning the closet 86
cleansing 94
colds 49
committed 76
conflicting messages 45
confused 45
confusing 26
conscious 123
consistent 95
cook 20
cooking 20, 21, 105
cooking classes 22
counselors 23

coupon 69
creativity 126
crisis 21

D

denial 52, 63, 80
depressed 84
depression 63
determination 29
diabetes 56
diarrhea 48
diet 96
digesting 26
dis-ease 74, 84
dis-eases 38, 60
doctors 14, 23
Dr. Anthony Satillaro 18
Dr. Bernie Siegel 52
Dr. Candace Pert, Ph.D. 40, 50
Dr. René Espy 24
dying 55
dysfunctional 46
dysfunctions 41

E

eating is 20
Eating Meditation 106
excellence 91
exceptional patient. 52
excuse 95
excuses 97
exercise 70, 81, 87, 94
exhaustion 49
experience 88

F

fat 113
fear 23, 55, 64, 80
fears 92
fine 80
flexibility 77
flow 118, 119
flu 49
focus 86
focused 98
food 87, 105, 106, 107
forgiveness 74, 75
forgiving 25, 46, 72
forty 17
Freda Fine 33, 51, 80
freedom 66
fruits 112

G

giving unconditionally 68
goals 92
God 23
good stress 78
Gracie Gossip 33, 35, 70
grains 113
grinding of teeth 49

H

happy 80
headaches 43, 48
healing 46, 72
health 87
healthy body 88
heart attack 49

high blood pressure 48, 60
humor 103, 104
hypertension 60
hypochondriac 42
hysterectomy 63

I

imagery 122
immune system 60, 124
indigestion 48
insomnia 48
intelligence 88, 125
intracellular communication
41
intuition 125

J

John Bradshaw 17
journey 84, 29
judgment 17
junk food 55

K

kinesiology 24

L

laugh 77, 102
laughter 71
ledge 89
leukemia 38
limits 55, 56
listen 73, 77, 80, 119
LOVE 45, 60, 64, 68

M

macrobiotic philosophy 19
macrobiotics 18
manifestation 73
medicine 71
meditate 81
meditation 70, 77, 82, 90, 106,
121, 122, 127
memories 78
memory 40
Micho Kishi 18, 19
mind 13, 106
molecules 40
multiple sclerosis 38
muscle aches 49
my cancer 40

N

Nanna Yabut 33, 54, 81
naturopathic doctors 23
negative 22
nineteen 15
nourishes 106
nourishment 106
Nurse Cratchit 33, 57, 77

O

opportunities 119
order blank 100
organic foods 20
our body 87

P

pain 24, 43
panic 89
peptides 41
perfect 59
perfection 57
perseverance 72
persistence 72
philosophy 22
positive 75, 103
possibilities 126
practice 72, 78, 127
practitioners 122
prescription 25
pressure 58
preventive 60
preventive practice 94
price 88, 116
procrastination 92

R

R.I.M. (Relaxation-Imagery-
    Meditation) 70, 65
relationships 87
relaxation 92, 109, 122
research 44
responsibility 39, 72, 104
responsible 40, 56
risk 38

S

saliva gland 15
seizures 49

self image 87
sexual dysfunction 48
silence 21
specific 92
spirit 22, 11, 64
spiritual 18, 21
spiritual awareness 126
spiritually 64
starving 23
stress 48, 123
stress related 48
stresses 78
subconscious mind 110
Super Stella 33, 47, 78
survival 52
survive 12

T

tapes 65
techniques 90
thankful 109
tobacco 113
tooth decay 56
transformation 27

U

ugly stress 79
ulcers 48
Ulla Dunnit 33, 39, 72
Universal Spirit 82, 129
unlimited possibilities 56

V

vegetables 105, 112

visualization 122
visualize 92
vitamin 113
vitamin C 114
vitamins 14

W

wake up call 86
Waukeen Wounded 33, 43,
    74
wellness 84

Y

yabut 54

Recent Releases from Awe Books Publishing

Books

Healthy Mind·Healthy Body: Using Your Mind Power to Stay Healthy and Overcome Illness.
By Judy Pearson
Easy to read and understandable, this book offers a common sense, sometimes humorous approach using your mind-body-spirit to stay well and overcome illness.
ISBN 0-9635179-0-2   160 pages, softcover $12.95

Meditations for the Time of Your Life
By Judy Pearson
Meditations for situations that come up in everyone's life.

Cassette Tape

Healthy Mind·Healthy Body: Using Your Mind Power to Stay Healthy and Overcome Illness.
By Judy Pearson
For your listening convenience. One side is verbal presentation and the other is a meditation.

How to Order:

Awe Books Publishing
2459 SE Tualatin Valley Hwy., #108
Hillsboro, Oregon 97123-7919
(503) 640-3208